Workplace Adventures

Tribulation and Triumph
on the Autism Spectrum

Chad Sides

Dragonswalk
Publishing

Also available from Chad Sides

Nonfiction:
Teaching the Wisemen

Tales of Horror:
The Nightmare After Christmas
If You Scream, You Will Die

Published in association with Dragonswalk Publishing.

Images Copyright © 2024
Cover art by Angel Nichols
angelwingsdesigner.wordpress.com

Printed in the United States of America.

ISBN 9798989946204

For the Smith twins, Stuart and Michael. I wonder how many of these stories you'll remember.

Table of Contents

Preface: My Job Log

I keep seeing clickbait collections of stories popping up all over social media: "Why I Quit my Job," "Demon Customers from Hell's Nightmare," and other things like that. Yes, I fall for the clickbait sometimes because those stories can be fun to read. I'm also a regular reader of notalwaysright.com which has user-submitted stories of bad customers (and bad employees on their sister site). They always make me think back on my own experiences because I've had some doozies myself, a few of which have even shown up on some of those sites.

I started writing a job journal (originally calling it my "Job Log") because I've been trying to do better with recording my memories. As age piles more experiences into one's brain, recalling details from long ago can become an ever-increasing challenge. Telling people that I almost owned a radio station or that I lived in some guy's basement while he employed cult-like tactics to keep me working for him tends to bring up questions that tickle my storybone (not unlike the standard funny bone). I figured if others were curious about what happened to me during those times, then I should write them down.

I had another, more introspective reason for this project: I'm on the autism spectrum, but I didn't learn that until later in life. I began to wonder what kind of impact autism might've had on my life before I knew it was a factor. This was an opportunity to examine my life through the lens of autism.

I didn't initially intend for this collection to become a book. It was an examination, maybe something I could pull from to create interesting social media posts or impart tidbits of wisdom when someone needed advice. As I wrote, I began to see a pattern that I never had before. My experiences, as wild and disjointed as they appear most of the time, tell a larger story - one that has more meaning than I would've ever realized if I hadn't started this project.

All my life I've heard "God works in mysterious ways." I was surprised to find out the Bible never says that. It most likely became a proverb thanks to a poem by William Cowper, but looking back at how one job somehow got me to another, I now see connections that show God's hand at work in some truly bizarre ways. As much as this is a collection of my strangest work experiences, it's also a story of God's hand in my life. As I connected those dots, I realized I had something more than a few social media posts; I had a story that others might appreciate. It's now become known as the book I wrote by accident.

I'm no expert on autism, but I have put effort into understanding how it affects how I operate on a mental and emotional level. I've been invited to speak on the topic several times and have had some success in helping people understand how we on the autism spectrum (I call us "auties") operate and helping fellow auties connect with the world around them.

We refer to it as a "spectrum" because of how vastly different we auties can be, functionality being just one facet of that. Many people don't even realize I'm autistic because my qualities are easy to overlook, especially for those that don't know me well and don't have much experience with autism. This is partly because I'm borderline, which basically means I've got enough of a foot in that world to understand it first-hand without dealing with the severity of challenges that some auties face. Meanwhile, other people may be affected so severely that they're rendered nonverbal and require a lot of help taking care of themselves. But it's not usually one extreme or the other. A great many people are in between with some leaning more towards independence while others need a little help.

We also don't always share the same traits. We do tend to share many commonalities, but I may react differently to certain situations than a person similar to me would. We tend to process information differently than the average person, and we can differ just as much from each other. Add comorbidities into the mix, and you've got a wide range of possibilities. As I recount my experiences, I'll hopefully be able to paint a picture of what life is like on the spectrum with insights on how another autie's experience might vary from mine.

Understanding how autism affects me gave me a new understanding of my life's journey. I may not have all the answers, but I invite you to join me in examining the part it played in my reactions and decisions in the hope that fellow auties and those who wish to understand them better can see something of themselves in my adventures (and avoid making the same mistakes that I did).

This is **not** a tell-all book. I won't sugar coat anything, but I'm definitely going to omit or change most of the names. You might be able to guess who a few of my employers were because I'm not going to be subtle with the clues. Just the same, some of what I experienced borders on illegal. I don't want to stir up trouble with claims I can't necessarily prove. I didn't pursue legal action then, and I don't plan to now; nor do I want anyone coming after me claiming libel or defamation. Having said that, everything I recount is completely true to the best of my recollection. I'm not going to fabricate anything for the sake of drama.

By the time this sees print, I'll have been at my current company for close to twenty years and doing the same job (more or less) for all but the first few of them. So, all the crap I gripe and complain about here ended up creating a good future for me. Without the hotel and chicken plant jobs (you'll hear all about those soon) I might never have ended up doing what I do now, so don't feel bad for me; it's all good. If a few of my tales leave you speechless like they did my wife, it will (SPOILER ALERT!!) get better by the last chapter. If God allows, I still have more stories to tell as I explore the world of publishing. Where I'll be a few years from now depends on factors I scarcely dare to dream about. For the next chapter, you'll have to find me and ask me.

Now settle in as we go way back. No, further back than that. Good heavens, I'm a child of the 80's, you have to go WAAAY back! That's more like it…

1

Sides Drywall

We're going to start with a story that's a little more sentimental than the others, because this is where everything began. My very first taxable job was with Sides Drywall. That's one name I don't have to change because it's my family's business. My uncle started the company back when I was a kid, got my dad (his brother) to join him, and has employed many family members at one time or another including me.

I've wondered if my dad hoped I would end up working with him there, maybe even taking his place. Sometimes I even wonder if maybe I should've stayed. I'm sure I could've done well enough there if I'd put my mind to it. Surely working with and for family would have its benefits, but I don't think it was ever my calling. Being where I am in Georgia has given me opportunities to get involved with cons like Dragon*Con and Con Nooga, which have been full of their own amazing experiences but more importantly opened the doors for me to meet my wife, get involved with Flickering Candle Productions' movies as an actor and producer, and discover Fans For Christ which I now help lead. (If you want to know more about what cons or Fans For Christ are, visit my appendices at the end of the book.)

I doubt any of that would've happened if I'd stayed in Alabama. I believe that by not going with the obvious choice of staying near home, I discovered possibilities that didn't exist there. There's probably a kernel of a story in that revelation alone.

Really, though, my disinterest in going into the family business started early. To get the full impact of what happened, I need to go back even further. Lest you think this book is going to be me complaining about other people, here I'm going to be telling on myself more than anyone.

In elementary school, I didn't have to study to get good grades. I was an avid reader, loved puzzles, studied dinosaurs to the point that I thought I wanted to become a paleontologist, and, in general, preferred cerebral activities to physical ones.

That worked against me because by the time I got to high school, I had terrible study habits. Algebra in particular was the bane of my existence. In later years, I did extremely well in Algebra 2 and Geometry, so looking back on it now I'm not sure

I know exactly what wasn't clicking for me. That's probably because it was a combination of factors rather than any single thing.

My first issue was a teacher that didn't connect with me. Think of it like someone trying to explain to you that the sky is blue, but you have no idea what he's talking about because the way he says it makes so little sense to you. That was me in Algebra class. Was my struggle my fault? I'm certainly not blameless, but across twelve grades of schooling and two degrees from two different colleges, I've never run across another teacher I had this much trouble following.

I remember having an especially hard time with word problems. English and Literature have always been my best subjects, so you might think that word problems would come easy to me. Yet somehow, a train leaving the moon at 3:00 last Wednesday with high winds at low tide and a bird flying to the Dead Sea from South Dakota on a north by northwest route at half gravity never seemed to be able to tell me how wide the color green was.

Whatever malfunction I had with this teacher, I admit that I was not a good student. I had no interest in math, much less Algebra, which meant I had no motivation to learn it. That might've been my worst subject, but it wasn't my only struggle; I also hated History. I don't mean to suggest that I have no interest in it at all; it's more accurate to say I hate how it's typically taught. Give me a David McCullough book that turns history into a story, and I'll learn, but give me a list of names and dates and you'll watch me fall asleep. Combine my disinterest with those bad study habits and the result was a horrible first year of high school.

I wasn't failing, but for the first time I wasn't excelling in school. I had to work at it. Trouble was, I didn't want to work at it. Auties like myself tend to hyperfocus on what interests us to the exclusion of everything else. I'm not as extreme with it as some are, but I still deal with it. To this day, I struggle with making myself accomplish things that are not within my interests. That's caused me unnecessary stress at work and sometimes results in me neglecting whole areas of my life if I don't force myself to pay attention. I have sleepless nights filled with dread over tasks I've left undone for too long and must deal with or face unpleasant consequences.

I am at least aware of my neglectful tendencies even though I still don't always do a great job of making myself do things when I should. However, in school all I knew was that I hated studying those subjects and wasn't good at them. I slipped from consistently being an above average student to average, at best.

I was already developing a severe lack of self-esteem because everyone around me was more athletic than I was, and now my academic struggles were making me feel dumb. My slipping grades both fueled and were fueled by a debilitating depression that affected my performance in all my subjects.

I wasn't good at anything. I voiced this lament to my cousin one summer day as we played basketball. She was a lot better than I was. She was better than me at most things... except chess - not that I always won (if anything we were evenly matched). She told me my problem was that I didn't practice enough. She was right, but there was underlying baggage there. I had fun playing ball with my friends and family, but I had no interest in the sport itself or desire to be part of a team. As is common with auties, I was also uncoordinated. I could fumble a football with glue on it.

If anyone one thing changed the course of my life at this point in time, it was karate. I began taking classes because I was tired of being bullied at school. Karate taught me how to fight and gave me the confidence to not use it if I didn't have to. Before I could drive a car, I had a black belt and was teaching others the martial arts. My accomplishments in karate fundamentally changed me in ways I don't think anyone could have ever predicted. Before long, I was keeping up with the more athletic kids in gym class. My body was stronger, and I had more confidence thanks to my progression.

One day at school, another boy tried to pinch my neck to make me squirm. I wrapped my arm around his, locked his elbow, and told him to leave me alone. He never bothered me again. I felt strong and capable like I never had before. It affected me in unexpected ways, too. I was a ticklish child - not so much after my training.

By the time I earned my black belt in Karate, my grades began improving - slowly at first then more rapidly. I eventually became an above-average student again, making grades that rivaled the top one or two percent of my school. Unfortunately, I still had more to learn by way of making bad decisions.

Riding confidently on my run of good grades, I made what was perhaps one of the dumbest decisions of my entire life. I chose to take a college level European history class.

I'm going to pause here for a second because, if you ever find yourself in my position, I don't want you to make the same mistake I did. Remember the lists I mentioned that put me to sleep? The worst of those are the repetitious British monarchy. I lose track of which George came after which Edward and where the Williams and the Victorias fall in with them. I couldn't care less which one of them did what. What's more, I don't care that I don't know. I don't want, need, or plan to gain that knowledge. I know that we won our independence as a nation from King George because my wife and I watch shows like *John Adams*, but I don't know which George he was. Even if I looked it up right now, I would forget it by tomorrow. But this is all information gained in hindsight. In high school I didn't realize how deep my disinterest ran or why.

So, what in the world would possess me to take a high-level European history class? I'll tell you what: peer pressure. I took it because my friends were. I got so bored that I made the single worst grade of my entire academic career. Then, as a result of having my confidence shaken, I shied away from taking the advanced English course that friends have told me they passed only because I helped them with it. I focused on the wrong thing for the wrong reason, and it held me back.

By the time I graduated, I was an excellent student with my first writing award, my first publication, and my first radio show. I'd decided to pursue a career in broadcasting, found a college, and earned a scholarship. I certainly ended on a high note. Getting to that point was a struggle that affected me for many years to come and involved a lot more than what I've recorded. Church and marching band certainly played roles in the story, as well. So did my first job.

I don't remember exactly when I made this decision, probably sometime during my trouble with Algebra, but I decided I didn't want to go to college at all because I didn't think I could do it. I no longer had any aspirations to be anything when I "grew up." I felt like I didn't have any talents, and I certainly didn't have any goals.

I thought I would join the military. I've never been a hunter, but my dad was so I grew up around guns and was comfortable with them. I figured at the very least I could follow orders, march onto a battlefield, and shoot someone. My dad, having been in the Navy during the Vietnam War, didn't want that for me so he devised a plan to change my attitude.

As soon as I was old enough, my parents told me I would be spending my summers working for Sides Drywall. I didn't have a choice. My dad had no intention of giving me a cushy office job. In fact, the exact opposite was true; I worked cleanup duty and stocked sheetrock. That means I was doing the hardest manual labor he could give me. I spent my days scraping dusty floors, shoveling piles of trash, and carrying heavy boards - the four foot by eight foot sheets of gypsum that are behind the paint or wallpaper of many modern American houses. The work was hard, the summers hot, and I wasn't ready to be out in the working world instead of enjoying my vacation time playing.

To make matters worse, the labor crew were not my kind of people. They were foul-mouthed and rough around the edges when I spent most of my time with church groups who didn't cuss or smoke. They didn't go easy on me because I was the boss' son, either - I wouldn't be surprised if my dad specifically told them not to. Not that they were mean to me, but that hardly mattered. I didn't like them, I didn't like the work, and I didn't want to be there. I resisted waking up in the early hours of the mornings to be at work on time, sulked in the truck while my dad drove us to the office, and interacted with my labor crew coworkers as little as I possibly could. I did my work, but always while griping and grumbling.

Over the next year or so, three significant changes occurred in me. First, I started realizing I was stronger than I thought I was. Carrying those sheetrock boards really wasn't as hard as I make it sound. I expected it to be taxing, so in my mind it was. What I didn't realize was that Karate had made my body strong enough to keep up with the older, larger men around me. The work was never easy, but I started seeing that I could handle it better than I expected to be able to.

Second, I had money in my pocket. I have to admit to going a little wild with spending my first couple of paychecks on too many cassette tapes. I was discovering heavy metal music and going a little bit overboard with it. My parents scolded me for buying so much ("You spent **how** much on tapes?"), but I had my first taste of earning money that I could spend on something I wanted.

Third, my dad showed me that I could find interesting people around me if I cared to look. One of his workers was a man we called Snake. This guy knew nunchuck moves that even my high-ranking senseis (teachers) didn't know. I've twirled nunchucks around my hands in ways I still rarely see to the delight of audiences at weapons demonstrations. Thanks to Snake and a Mexican preacher who would talk to me about the Bible during our lunch breaks, I started getting to know the people around me more instead of judging them.

I grew up enough that my dad took me off the labor crew and started teaching me how to do more complicated jobs. Most of the time, I was helping him install drop ceilings. Those are the kind that have a suspended metal frame with tiles inserted. I still got the grunt work portion of the job - opening and distributing materials, fetching tools, that sort of thing. It wasn't glamorous, and when the work got repetitive it could be quite boring. Still, it was better than hauling sheetrock boards all day. That's not to say that I started enjoying any of it, I just didn't hate it quite as intensely as before.

My dad liked to joke with the guys working for him saying, "If I get ahead of you, you're fired." A few times he would start to say that to me then stop and say, "No, not you." I think he was afraid I might take him up on it! Even so, my attitude improved to the point that some of the guys actually liked working with me. That alone encouraged me to be less of a grouch on the job, even when the early mornings and sweaty labor had me wishing I was at home.

When my grades and confidence began to improve again, I started thinking college wasn't such a bad idea if it meant not having to work in construction. I left home for life at a university immediately after high school with a career path that had me excited and hopeful.

Only once since then have I worked a job as hard as the backbreaking labor of hanging ceilings, stuffing insulation, and handling drywall. Most of my time has been spent behind computers or mixing boards for radio and TV stations. Even so, the smells of any construction site remind me of the days I spent working with my dad. I had it better than I thought I did back then. Considering some of the crazy stories I have to tell, that was actually one of the best working environments I've ever had; I just didn't have the real-life what-is-wrong-with-this-world type of experiences to appreciate it yet.

2

The Inspiration Station

I got my first taste of the inner workings of a radio station when my youth pastor took a group of us kids on a sort of field trip. He had a show on a small Southern Gospel station, WDVI, that was popular among the local churches and thought we would enjoy observing what he did there. He was right. I just about fell over myself checking out all the mixing boards with their rows of sliders and knobs, the microphones, the tape decks stacked on top of other tape decks, machines that played cartridges that resembled 8-tracks but for which I had no name, and, of course, the racks full of music.

Something else about that work appealed to me, although I didn't realize it at the time. The DJ was in a room all by himself. Everyone else had to stay out or at least be very quiet. The isolation of the booth called out to me. I didn't know why it did,

I just knew that I wanted it. Little did I know that I would soon be spending a night each and every week in that booth for over a year.

My first impression of the radio station was that it was too complicated for me. The job demands a lot of attention. You have to know which slider or knob to move when, how to cue a song on a tape (CDs would soon simplify that, but even they had to be set properly to play the right audio at precisely the right moment), how each and every machine worked, and where to look if something didn't work, all while keeping an audience entertained. It seemed like a lot.

It **was** a lot! But my initial impression of being overwhelmed by all the buttons gave way to a craving to be the one pushing those buttons when I took a second trip to the station the next year.

By the time I was sixteen with my own car, I'd achieved the rank of black belt in my Karate class. I felt like I was good at something perhaps for the first time since the days when the adults in my life had praised my encyclopedic knowledge of dinosaurs. I can't remember exactly when my success with writing comedic poetry began, but it was shortly before or shortly after this point in time. People I barely knew would approach me to tell me how much they liked my poem "An Ode to Prune Juice." Such praise boosted my confidence beyond anything I'd ever felt before. Depression still weighed me down, but it came in waves instead of being a constant state of mind.

I say all that because if I'd been in the same mental and emotional state that I had been at fourteen or fifteen, I'm not sure that I would've had any aspirations for my own radio show. As an older teen who was finally seeing himself in a positive light, I believed I could do it and wanted it badly enough to make it my primary goal in life.

I couldn't have cared less about Southern Gospel music. I still can't. I despise the twangy sounds of country music, and Southern Gospel is everything I don't like about the genre taken to the next level. The only time I listened to WDVI was during one of their rare, late-night rock shows. When I say they played rock, I'm talking about the poppy, mainstream sounds of artists like Steven Curtis Chapman and Michael W. Smith. Even the melodic sounds of metal bands like Stryper and Whitecross were too edgy for this station, never mind the heavily distorted, angry style of bands like Vengeance Rising and The Lead. My appreciation for those heavier bands would soon develop into a lifelong obsession, but I cut my Christian rock teeth on Carman and DeGarmo & Key. They were why I cared about hearing any music on a religious radio station in the first place.

I talked the DJ of WDVI's first, and at the time only, rock show into putting me on the air and letting me dedicate DeGarmo & Key's song "Don't Stop the Music" to the station's staff. It was my very first time speaking over radio airwaves. If I had any doubts about wanting to be on the radio, hearing my voice come out of my speakers removed them. I immediately started researching what it would take to make that dream happen.

My best friend Stuart Smith was interested in radio as well. We became a team as we applied for a license from the FCC (Federal Communications Commission) and approached the owner of WDVI. He was willing to consider us if we proved ourselves capable.

Our friends Mike and Johnny had beaten Stuart and me to the punch as far as getting their own show, which worked out well for us because we were able to tag along with them to learn how all the equipment worked. Their show "Powerhouse" (named after the White Heart song) aired one night a week. We observed them for a few nights then guest hosted a couple of times. It was the most fun I'd ever had sitting in a chair.

Stuart and I began preparing for our first show by taking inspiration from the "Powerhouse" name and settling on a theme song. Carman's album *Addicted to Jesus* had come out not long before. We liked the title song and thought the theme was appropriate for the show we wanted to do, so we settled on "A2J" as our name. The "Powerhouse" team took a night off and gave "A2J" their slot - with managerial permission, of course.

I still have a recording of that very first show. It's amusing to listen to how young we sounded. We sounded like amateurs. Of course, that's exactly what we were… and yet we managed to sound like we knew what we were doing (at least a little).

Over the course of the next year and a half we would become a regular show every other week, then a weekly program, then WDVI's flagship rock show. That last part sounds more glamorous than it really was. We were, in fact, the only rock show for a while. I doubt many people were beating down WDVI's doors to be a rock DJ on a Christian station. Even though we were given a late-night time slot, we were still given two hours to fill with the least edgy Christian rock we could find. I got into trouble more than once for playing something that was too heavy for the station's primary audience, with my biggest reprimand coming after playing a punk song by Crashdog.

Sides Drywall, who'd already been advertising on the station, and the Lighthouse Christian bookstore in Auburn became our top supporters. My dad asked me if I would create a new commercial spot for the station to use. I'd been dabbling in audio editing ever since I'd first set my sights on working in radio, so I used what I learned to create a spot that I'm still very proud of. Stuart and I wrote a script, chose some background music, and locked ourselves in the recording booth at the station until we had something professional enough for WDVI to continue using for many years after "A2J" had broadcast our final show.

My time as part of the A2J Crew remains one of the highlights of my entire life. I'm proud of what we learned, what we accomplished, and the immense enjoyment of the whole experience. Not everyone liked us, though. Some of the

Southern Gospel DJs (I never knew exactly who) would stay up late to listen to our show, then immediately complain to management who would get on to us if we stepped out of line even a little. One of them heard me mix a laugh track from another show into one of the songs I played and angrily demanded that I keep my hands off anything that wasn't my own. I didn't think anyone would care as long as I put everything back as I found it. Obviously, I was wrong. Although the territorial attitude confused me, it did push me to start experimenting with my own sounds and mixes.

Management liked us, otherwise they wouldn't have given us a time slot (we had enough listener and monetary support to give them justification for keeping us around), but they also had to keep their broader audience and their more popular DJs happy. Sometimes we probably deserved a reprimand, like my stunt playing a punk song which I knew full well would get me in trouble (it was worth it). Other times, I felt like our critics tolerated us only because they couldn't get rid of us. One conversation proved that they were going to complain about us even if we behaved:

Management: "Did you play anything out of the rotation last night?" (The rotation was the approved list of music, a playlist written on paper, from which we were allowed to choose our songs.)

Me: "No, I don't think so. No, I'm certain that we didn't."

Management: "You're sure you didn't play any songs not

in the rotation?"

Me: (I had to think about it, because if there was one rule I didn't follow it was sticking to songs approved by the station. I at least had enough sense to not push my luck too frequently with that. I'd gotten us in trouble a couple of weeks before, so I was on a streak of following the rules... at least for a while.) "I'm certain we didn't."

Management: "Because we got a complaint about a song you played. We're going to have to review the rotation."

I never did find out which song earned us a complaint, but I realized at that point that even when we followed the rules certain people were still going to look for ways to get us in trouble. I don't know if they wanted us off the air entirely or if they just wanted to keep us as tightly restrained as they possibly could.

Either way, we probably had a conversation like that at least once a month. Stuart was to blame occasionally, but he'd begun gravitating more towards the mainstream pop and country sounds that WDVI's audience preferred, so if he deviated from our rock music format it was usually to play something more acceptable to a wider audience. I was the one pushing boundaries as I discovered more punk and heavy metal bands. Church society as a whole was very much in its "all rock music is of the Devil" heyday so if anyone was getting us into trouble for playing songs too heavy for WDVI's airwaves, it was most likely me.

Not all of our complaints came through management, though. "A2J" was a call-in show. We frequently played requests and dedications. Our typical format was that we would both open and close the show. Most of the rest of our two hours was trading off microphone duties while the other took phone calls and hunted the requested music. Listeners would sometimes call in to educate us on the evils of rock music.

One such call came while we were playing Petra's song "I Love the Lord." The call came as a shock to me because while the song is energetic with loud guitars, the lyrics are easy to understand and about as solidly Christian as you can get: "Gonna say it loud, gonna say it proud / Hey! I, I love the Lord!"

The caller started with this question: "Do you really think this kind of music is going to save someone's soul?" He went on to tell me why he threw away his Carman tape. He didn't like the song "Witch's Invitation," a song about Carman's fictional confrontation with a warlock that was reportedly based on a real experience of his friend Mario Murillo's. The song is all about how following the Devil leads to destruction while Jesus rescues us from darkness, but since it involved a "witch," it was an evil song that this listener couldn't stand having in his presence. He told me how when he heard the song, he yanked the cassette out of his car's tape deck and threw it out the window even though he liked all of Carman's other songs. I should've asked him why he didn't do the same with his Bible since it mentions witches, demons, and even Satan himself.

Expecting his story to convince me that the song, and by association every other song on the album, was tainted by evil he preached to me about how all Christian music should be Southern Gospel, and why God didn't like rock. The only thing of which he convinced me was that he was mentally unstable, which I myself would surely be if forced to listen to nothing but Southern Gospel music.

I heard arguments ranging from "they don't say the name of Jesus enough on their album" to "the beat comes from African voodoo rituals" to "what kind of name is One Bad Pig for a Christian to use?" I often felt personally attacked when someone tried to educate me on the evils of rock music because it always came with an attitude of "you're a bad Christian if you listen to this." It wasn't just about me, though. I had a lot of respect for many of the artists in the industry as well as for people like Pastor Bob Beeman who worked with the bands behind the scenes. I felt a need to come to their defense.

In some ways dealing with these critics was preparing me for life as an adult autie. I find that many of us are easily offended by the use of terminology we don't like and have little patience for statements or questions arising from misconceptions like "you don't look autistic." This is not at all unique to us; I see that behavior in many other communities as well, more often and far more severe in some cases, but use a term like "high functioning" and prepare to feel the wrath of the autism community. Many will do everything they can to make you feel like the worst scum of the universe. That sort of behavior is why I avoid most online autistic groups.

I take a different approach. I try to educate as much as I can, which is the very attitude that motivates me to write so much about the reality I've experienced. I also try not to judge based on well-meaning terminology and concepts. Knowledge of autism and how it works has been an ever-changing field of study since it started. When I was a baby, my parents knew there was something different about me. I didn't behave like other kids. But they didn't have a name for what set me apart.

When I was in college, I took part in a psychological experiment. When the professor talked to me about the results, he told me that my logic, while accurate, was reversed from how most people think. I found that interesting, but I thought that just made me quirky; I had no reason to explore the possibility of that being related to autism because all that was in the public mind at the time was the idiot savant portrayals in the movies.

When I took my first autism test, I was given the specific classification of Asperger's Syndrome. Now, the diagnosis of Asperger's is part of the autism spectrum rather than a separate diagnosis.

When so much is changing as we learn more about how autism works, I don't expect everyone around me to know the latest information and theories. We can't all be experts, especially when it comes to those with no direct connection. I think back on how what I thought of autism was wrong for so long. I think about how little I know of Down's Syndrome because I have no reason to invest time into learning more. Why should I judge people who are in the same position when it comes to autism, especially if I have the opportunity to teach them something about it?

People in general are annoyingly easy to offend. I like to say that people are butts looking for a reason to hurt. If we are always in a constant state of anger over perceived offenses, we'll never be able to communicate effectively. These were the lessons I first began learning in response to Christians treating me like I was going to Hell because I liked a particular genre of music. I began learning how to respond with a considered argument instead of trading attack for attack. That caused me to become obsessed with proving my point when I thought someone was wrong, but it was because I wanted to be right not because I was offended. I've had to learn to make my point and let things go.

Far from driving me away from Christian rock, the more I defended myself against criticisms for it the more invested in our show I became. I loved the creativity involved with producing promotional spots to play on my show. I loved the focus that running the equipment required. I loved being behind the microphone. And I loved that I was dealing mostly with technology instead of people. Because of all that, I decided that I wanted to work in broadcasting for the rest of my life. I found a university with a communications program that included broadcasting and left home to learn how to start a career in radio.

Our final "A2J" show was emotional and fun. We turned it into a party with several of our friends joining us at the station. We let our friends introduce songs and sent out many dedications to the listeners who supported us over the years. We gave away tapes and CDs to callers, reflected back on our early days, and spoke about our plans for the future. It was as perfect a final show as I could have imagined.

Unfortunately, my last interaction with the station before moving off to college left a bad taste in my mouth. The university had a radio station - WRAM because the school mascot was a ram. I'd already made plans to get involved with it as soon as classes began. This was a very small station with a broadcast range not much larger than the campus itself. It had a library of music, but it amounted to a few dozen CDs and a few vinyl records. I was used to having a room full of music with new releases coming in on a regular basis. How was I going to be able to have a good show if I hardly had any music to play? Would people listen if I didn't have the latest, greatest radio hits? I saw the lack as a problem that I could help solve. I decided I wanted to be proactive.

I began by researching how to get music from record labels and making contacts. My intention was to get WRAM as a station on the mailing lists of whomever was responsible for sending out the music. What I discovered was that they all wanted a specific point of contact. I didn't have that information about the campus station yet, so I used myself - making sure to be upfront about the fact that I didn't work at that station yet, but that I was gathering music to take with me. In a few months' time, I'd amassed a stack of CDs that equaled probably a third of what the station currently had on hand.

A couple of weeks before I moved away for college with stacks of CDs in hand to offer and to use for the show I hoped to soon have, I got a call from one of the WDVI DJs I'd considered as a mentor. He was the person I'd first spoken to about how to get record labels to send me music, which is how he knew to talk to me about it now. For the sake of this part of the story I'll call him "David" because I'm listening to a David Arkenstone song while I write:

David: What did you do with all of the CDs you got?

Me: I'm taking them with me to the college station.

David: No, you need to bring them here.

Me: But I got them specifically for the college station to use.

David: The money for those CDs comes out of the artists' pockets.

Me: I told them I was taking the stuff they sent me with me to the new station, and they sent me all this for that purpose.

David: You need to bring them here. Anything you paid money for you can keep.

Looking back on it now, I wish I'd stood my ground. I

don't know what David thought I was intending to do with the music because he acted like I was trying to steal something. Did he think I was being dishonest, that I was taking all the music home to keep for myself? A fair amount of it was stuff I didn't even like. I can't help but wonder now about the honesty of his own intentions. If he really was concerned about the artists' money, wouldn't it make more sense to give the music to a radio station that needed it instead of a station that already had more than it used? On top of that, a significant portion of what I'd gathered was rock. With "Powerhouse" and "A2J" both off the air, WDVI no longer had a flagship rock show. If they ever had another one after us, I never heard about it.

In my mind, as I imagine the way I wish the conversation had gone, I tell David that I'd amassed this collection with the expressed intent of using it at WRAM. That's what the label who sent me the music expected me to do with it so that's what I was going to do with it. I didn't consider that if I refused to comply, he had no recourse other than trying to make me feel guilty. If I'd taken more time to think about it, I would've realized that I had nothing to feel guilty about.

I wanted to remain on good terms with WDVI. I didn't know if I would need connections there as I pursued a career in radio, and I was still friends with the owner, office staff, and some of the other DJs. I didn't want any of them to think I was being underhanded in my dealings with them or the record labels. I did defy David on one count: I was absolutely not going to give him the heavy metal music that was going to end up going straight to WDVI's garbage can. I boxed up everything else and dropped it off at the station. I never saw or spoke to David again after that.

Three things bothered me about that situation. First of all, David's reasoning never made sense to me. Now that I have a degree in broadcasting and have worked as a DJ at a handful of different radio stations and clubs (some of them Christian focused, some of them not), his reasoning still doesn't make sense. Secondly, I felt like I'd put a lot of effort into a plan to help the campus station but ended up with very little to show for it. I did come away with a few heavy metal samplers which I was able to use, but that was hardly the windfall of popular music I'd had in hand for the station to add to their daily rotation.

Lastly, I was mad at myself for giving in so easily. I had a defensible position for which I could've fought harder. The more I dwelt on the first two points, the more I kicked myself for giving in.

Most of my memories of WDVI are great ones. I still listen to recordings of some of my old shows and laugh at how young Stuart and I sound. We were often corny, but we did some good work there of which I can be proud. Even if nobody other than our families still remember "A2J," it was an experience worth having. In some ways, it changed the course of my life. Was it a good change? That depends on how you look at what was yet to come.

3

Fast Food Bag Boy

After a year or two in college, when I still lived on campus and had to go home for the summers, I got a job working with fast food: Taco Bell. My favorite thing on the menu at that time was the Meximelt (which was discontinued some years ago). The best part about working there was making myself the most fantastic Meximelts in the history of mankind. Oh, how I miss those.

Much to my surprise, I don't have many good stories from working at the Bell. That's the only reason I'm not omitting their name. Since what I have to say about them is that they were a good employer and I eat more of their Mexican pizzas than I should (and chili cheese burritos when I can find them), I hope they won't mind me mentioning them.

As far as customer service jobs go, it was pretty decent. I had a good boss who liked me, no confrontations with insane customers, and no real complaints about my time there. The worst I ran into was clashing with one of the more senior employees because she wanted me to always do things exactly her way. What did I know? I was the new kid, so I did my best to acquiesce even when I thought the demands were unnecessary. Even that wasn't so bad, though. Her demands weren't unreasonable - nothing like "go clean the grease trap out with your tongue" or "take the toilet outside and hose it down." It was typically more like "you're supposed to mop the floor from left to right not right to left."

Since I wouldn't challenge her on her demands, our boss finally had to tell her to leave me alone because I was doing a good job. She eventually lightened up and we actually became friends. She even came to me for relationship advice. I couldn't tell you why; I couldn't seem to hang on to a girlfriend for more than a couple of months during those days so I knew less about love than I did about which direction I should be mopping the floor.

My one jaw-dropping moment at the Bell was when a customer, standing in front of the counter with the menu clearly visible, asked if we sold tacos. How do you answer that and remain professional? With snarky replies flashing through my brain one after the other, I replied with a simple "Yes, ma'am."

This story is not about the Bell, though, it's about a

grocery store that I probably shouldn't name. For all the good things I have to say about working at Taco Bell, they didn't provide me with enough hours, pushing me to take a second job at a well-known supermarket. This place was not so accommodating.

I've had far worse jobs since then. The work wasn't anywhere near as hard as my construction experience, and nobody was incompetent or hateful. I would say that alone makes it better than many jobs. At the same time, if there was a task nobody else wanted to do and it fell anywhere near my regular job responsibilities, I was the one doing it. The good news was that bathrooms were somebody else's job, but anything to do with the parking lot was all me. I could be in the middle of doing a task my boss had already given me and he would still randomly pull me away to go clean up trash in the parking lot or scrub the sidewalk or whatever else caught his eye. The only time I could guarantee not being interrupted was if I was helping a customer. Nothing was more important than that.

Buggies (that's what we call shopping carts here in the South) were the second most important part of my job. Rain or shine doesn't cut it. If God sent the seventh plague of hail and fire, I was expected to be out in it collecting those buggies. Our parking lot is connected with a strip mall on one side and a fast-food place on the other. All combined, it was a huge lot. People rarely (if ever) parked very far away, but they certainly didn't mind leaving buggies where they could roll a hundred yards in almost any direction, which is exactly what they tended to do if the wind picked up enough.

Having to chase buggies all the way to the strip mall - sometimes to the second or third store - was bad enough, but walking down to the busy street in front of the parking lot was far worse. I could envision one of those buggies making it into the street, where it would surely cause a wreck. They never made it past the grass and trees, but it would've been up to me to retrieve them if they ever had gotten that far. My other fear with being so close to the road was that some absent-minded driver would run me down while pulling into the parking lot. People don't watch where they're going.

I wasn't hired specifically to be a buggy boy. That was just one of the duties of being a bag boy. That was my prime directive. I was expected to know how to properly bag groceries because, let me tell you, there certainly was a proper way. We were trained on it. To this day I'm picky about what I have in a bag with my cans, having non-food items in with the food, and making sure eggs and bread are set apart. I guess I was either lucky or I got it right, because I never had a complaint even from the pickiest of customers. I can also be somewhat OCD about how I sort things (one look at my music library is usually enough to make people wonder what's wrong with me) so that may have worked in my favor without me even realizing it.

These were the days before self-checkout, which means we had a full complement of cashiers, and those were almost entirely young, cute girls. That alone was worth working as a bag boy. I would float amongst them bagging groceries as they scanned them, prioritizing customers by the size of their orders and how much they looked like they might need help, but also by how cute I thought the cashier was. That last part didn't affect me as much as I make it sound, as there wasn't one among them that I wouldn't have taken out. That all stopped when a friend I'd known in high school came through my line one day so that she could ask me out. We dated for the rest of the summer, so I quit caring so much about the cashiers at least in a flirtatious way.

The biggest problem I had at the store was that my boss was oblivious when it came to making the schedules. I explained to him when I took the job that I was already working at Taco Bell, which he acknowledged to my face and then immediately discarded. As far as he was concerned, I was to adhere to his schedule first, and if I could squeeze in some time to work my other job outside of that then that was fine and dandy.

That was no big deal for a while, since he tended to work me during the busy daylight hours. As the weeks went by, I fell into a comfortable pattern. I could get from the store to the Bell in less than two minutes, so I actually liked it when my schedules butted up against each other. I spent many of my days getting to the store in the morning, working my five or six hours, changing into my Taco Bell uniform in the bathroom, making a Chad-masterwork Meximelt or two for lunch, and serving tacos until time to go home.

At some point, as if sensing he'd been making my life too easy, my grocery store boss started mixing up my schedule. My Taco Bell manager was willing to work with me if I could get her my store schedule, but my other boss was notorious for waiting until the last minute to post his latest jumble. It got bad enough that I almost got fired from the Bell. If my boss had liked me any less than she did, she might not have worked so hard to keep me around.

Somehow, we found a way to make it work. I don't know now how I managed it other than being willing to take the most undesirable shifts at the Bell to leave as much time open as possible during the busiest hours at the grocery store. It's funny how shuffling two jobs and a girlfriend was manageable at that age when it seems like I can't find enough hours in the day now despite working only a single job and living in the same house as my wife. I didn't appreciate how free I was at that age compared to the responsibilities of being an adult.

At the end of the summer, it was time to move back to college. That meant quitting both jobs. Taco Bell was sad to see me go and said I would have a job there if I ever wanted to return. The supermarket… well, that's where I got a small measure of retribution for almost getting me fired with those roll-of-the-dice schedules.

Both employers knew that my time there would be only for the summer. Even so, I gave them each more than two weeks' notice in writing and in person. I wanted to leave on the best terms possible both for the sake of references and in case I was back the next summer needing a job again.

Knowing how oblivious to his employees' lives my supermarket boss was, I looked at the schedule for the week following my last day. Sure enough, there I was slated for my regular shift - as regular as it got for me that is. I've always felt that was confirmation that he was never malicious in his scheduling, and I know from other interactions that he wasn't incompetent; he simply didn't care or didn't pay attention to anything other than putting names into time slots. Feeling like I'd done my due diligence in handing in my notice in writing, I took some pleasure in not showing up for work that next Monday.

I hear "everyone should have to work customer service once in their life" a lot. That's not a bad idea. When you know what someone goes through in a job like that, you tend to have more patience with them. Chasing buggies down to a busy street keeps me mindful of putting mine back where they aren't going to roll all over the place. I got out of fast food virtually unscathed, and it still left an impression on me.

I like to think I would treat service workers well just because that's the kind of guy I am, but even people I know to be good natured and kindhearted can throw some rage around when things don't go right for them. I do have my limits - don't give me someone else's food and then argue with me about what

I ordered when I say it's wrong (I'll talk about that more in a later story), because I can't be bullied into slinking off with my tail between my legs thankful that I got half the food I paid for. But stuff happens, people make mistakes, and as long as they're willing to correct those mistakes, screaming about it and throwing things around like a spoiled child doesn't make anyone's life better. There's your moral of today's story.

4

Electric Retail

When I got an apartment with some of the guys I knew from school, I decided it was time to find a local job rather than going back to my parents' between semesters. I began hunting for steady employment that wouldn't interfere with my classwork and was soon hired by a well-known electronics retailer.

The company treated me well enough. Even when we did have to follow ridiculous requirements (like asking every customer their name and address for our mailing list) we weren't pushed beyond reason on such things. We could get in trouble if we didn't ask for the information, but nobody expected us to be able to get it from everyone.

I've heard horror stories about rewards programs and credit cards at other companies - employees reprimanded, even yelled at, if they didn't sign up enough new customers. We only had extended warranties that we were expected to offer, but the company was never overly pushy about them and my managers were never unreasonable. Employees were incentivized to sell them by way of commissions, so I always made sure to offer them in hopes that I'd get lucky, but once they declined I was happy to let the matter drop. Nobody yelled at me if I went a month without selling a warranty.

I didn't hate my time selling electronics. It was a relatively low-pressure environment, a fact that I would come to appreciate later when food in my stomach depended entirely upon me selling enough merchandise to make a profit. (Yes, you're going to read all about that later). At the store, though, I got paid even if I sold nothing at all. I doubt I would've lasted long if I wasn't selling anything, but I could still afford to put gas in the car to get to work if I had a bad week. Commissions kept us motivated to do well, but we didn't live or die by them.

Be that as it may, I am not a good salesman. Even as a writer I struggle with selling myself and my work. Combine my autism (which means I don't do as well with body language or social situations as the average person) with me being introverted (which means I need more time away from people than with them, even when those times are good) and having little patience when it comes to people being dumb or inconsiderate and you've got yourself someone who is better off in a job that doesn't involve a lot of personal interaction.

One of the reasons I like writing is one of the same reasons I liked working as a DJ on the radio: it involves a lot of solitude. That's not to say I don't enjoy interacting with people, I just prefer it in small doses and when it doesn't involve me trying to convince someone to do or buy anything.

My saving grace at the electronics store was that I'm good with technology. At one point, I had the highest number of computer sales in our district (even when up against the much larger stores) because I was good at explaining functions and answering questions. It had less to do with me convincing people they needed something and more to do with me knowing what would accomplish whatever need they had.

One of the most amusing interactions I ever had I think illustrates my salesmanship, or lack thereof. We were coming up on the Christmas season and had lots of gadgets aimed at children. One of those was a simple laptop computer designed for kids learning how to read. I don't remember now all of the functions it offered, but one I will never forget cost me a sale.

A woman came into the store looking for possible presents for her kid. She noticed the laptops and began asking me about them. I showed her how to turn on the display model. As she poked around the functions, she came across one that dealt with past tense verbs. It would offer the present tense and the user would type in the appropriate past tense version. It even offered a blank space for each letter of the correct answer.

Her word was "blow," so the screen read "What is the

past tense of blow? _ _ _ _ "

The woman conferred with her companion for a second and then tried to enter "blowed."

What should I do? Should I correct her? The customer is always right, right? Except that the children's laptop was already telling her she was wrong, so would I really be at fault?

After a moment's hesitation, I corrected her hoping she would laugh it off as a momentary mental lapse, what we used to call a "brain fart." "No, ma'am," I said, "It's 'blew.'"

To my horror, she attempted to type in "B L U E."

Before I could correct her again, which I fully intended to do, she handed me the laptop saying, "This is too hard."

"It's not hard! Just because you don't know elementary grammar doesn't mean your kid shouldn't learn!" That's what I wanted to say as I watched my commission walk out the door.

I've dwelt on that moment over and over trying to figure out how I could've turned that situation into a sale. Maybe I'm being too hard on myself. Maybe by then it was a lost cause for anyone, but I can't help thinking that a better salesperson than I could do it. I'm glad I no longer have to.

I served a lot of customers during my time, including some of our local celebrities: news anchors and the like. Most were pleasant enough. We had a few regulars and good rapport with them. Every once in a while, though, we'd get the types that make these stories fun to tell.

Store policy was that we wouldn't accept personal

checks that didn't have the account holder's information printed on them. Every time I've opened a bank account and gotten the starter checks, I've worried that they would be useless until my regular checks came in. It feels like punishment for no reason other than being new.

The thing is, there was a good reason for our policy: scammers. When I was young and naïve, I didn't appreciate the lengths to which some people will go to take advantage of some young cashier who can be easily intimidated or bamboozled. That's why you always announce out loud the amount of cash the buyer hands you and don't put it away until the transaction is complete. Just recently I handed someone a $100 bill, and I, as the buyer, got nervous when she didn't say, "Out of a hundred." If she handed me the wrong change and I corrected her, would I be accused of trying that very scam? Nothing like that happened, but until I had the correct change in hand, I was nervous.

One customer attempted to make a purchase with starter checks. I was behind the counter, but it was my manager who was making the sale. Being polite and professional, but unwavering, he let the customer know that we couldn't accept his check. I certainly can't recall the exact exchange now, but the conversation went something like this:

"I'm good for it. I promise," he said.

"It's company policy. I can't accept checks without your name and information printed on them," my manager replied.

"I have plenty of money," the customer retorted.

"We can take a card or cash if you want to hit an ATM," my manager said.

After a few failed attempts to talk us into taking his check the customer got belligerent.

"I have more money in my account than you make in a year!" He yelled.

"Then you shouldn't have any trouble with coming up with another form of payment."

"You **will** take my check, or I will have your job!" he screamed.

"Chad, call the police," my manager instructed me.

I thought it was a bluff. I expected the customer to back off once I picked up the phone. He didn't, but I hesitated long enough to give my manager time to run him off.

After the customer left my manager turned to me. He wasn't angry, but he also wasn't exactly pleased. "Chad, next time I tell you to call the police you pick up the phone and dial 911 right then."

I never had to deal with that situation again, but having had time to reflect on it I recognized the likelihood of that customer being a thwarted scammer trying to bully us into his scheme. I guess it's possible that an honest man would be angry enough to yell at us, but if he'd had as much money as he claimed he should've been able to find another method of payment. If he was passing bad checks, he only had the one option.

Being yelled at was harrowing; somehow being cussed out was not. One evening, when the sun had gone down and the clock counted the minutes to closing time, I was starting to think I'd seen my last customer for the day. I was entrusted with the keys to the store by this time, so it was up to me to close down and lock up. Everyone else had gone home for the day since we all expected this night to be as uneventful as they usually were.

A man of maybe forty, give or take a few years, entered the store. I greeted him as we were expected to do with every customer and asked if he needed help finding anything. If he said anything at all I don't remember what it was, but it was obvious that he didn't want my help, so I said, "Let me know if you need anything" and left him alone.

I waited at the front counter for him to return until two older ladies, probably both around seventy, entered and headed straight to me with a question. They were looking for something I knew was out of stock, but we'd just gotten a shipment which very likely included what they were wanting. I checked to see that the man was still off hunting whatever it was he was after, dragged our box of new items into the hallway where it wouldn't be in anyone's way but would allow me a clear line of sight to the front of the store, and began digging through it.

After a minute or two, I looked up to see the man standing at the register. I immediately excused myself, telling the ladies that I would be back with them momentarily, and rushed back to the front counter. This was a small store so my walk from the hallway to the register once I saw the man standing there was less than thirty seconds and my total time helping the two ladies was less than five minutes.

Before I even reached the register, I began speaking with the intention of conveying that this man's purchase was my top priority. "I'm sorry for the wait. Did you find everything OK?"

His reply was a profanity laden tirade about how he'd been waiting at the counter for ten minutes.

I don't remember my exact words, but they were something to the effect of "I'm sorry for the wait, but please watch your language. We have other customers."

I rang up his purchase and took his money as he continued to berate me with the harshest language.

"You know what? I'm sorry, but I offered to help you when you walked in the door, and you brushed me off. These two nice ladies did need my help so what was I supposed to do, tell them I couldn't help them because I had to stand here in case you came back at some point? I came over here the second I saw you standing here, and you weren't here for ten minutes because you haven't even been in the store for ten minutes."

I'm pretty sure that most businesses don't allow their employees to tell off their customers in such a way. I'm probably lucky that nobody was there to hear me. I guess I felt emboldened by the way my manager had stood up to the Check Bully.

He stormed off still spouting profanities while yelling that he was never coming back to this so-and-so store. I yelled back, "Thank God for that!" I was tense, maybe even a little shaky as I can get during a confrontation, but I would not be cussed out by a customer being a jerk no matter what the consequences might have been.

As the man shoved his way through the door, I apologized to the two ladies. Before I could get the words out, all three of us cracked up. I'm not sure if Cussing Man heard us or not, but we probably laughed for two minutes before we regained our composure and I was able to help them find what they needed. I was grateful to them for being pleasant and good natured about the whole incident. I felt a lot better about the night because of them.

We had the occasional angry customer, but only a few stand out as being unreasonable, Cussing Man being among the worst I ever encountered. Dealing with these situations gave me an understanding of what people in retail go through. The customer is not always wrong; there are certainly times when the employee is the one at fault - like the drive-thru worker who argued with me about what I'd ordered. I'd ordered food for two, but he was giving me only a single sandwich. When I told him that was wrong and repeated my order, he replied, "No, you only ordered one."

Even if he'd been correct and I'd been the one who had goofed, that put me in a bind. Either my wife or I wouldn't be getting fed. I wasn't about to let my wife go without, and I'm prone to get hangry (hungry to the point of getting angry) so feeding me is in everyone's best interest. I needed to find a resolution. I saw no reason why finding one should prove difficult for us.

My confidence in an easy solution faded the longer we went back and forth about it. Finally, I suggested that I would pay whatever the difference was if he would simply double my order. At that point, I didn't care which one of us was wrong, I didn't even care if I was going to get the right sandwich; all I cared about was leaving with food for two.

Rather than respond to my request in any way, he repeated that I'd only ordered one sandwich like he expected me to admit he was right and drive away with what he'd decided to allow me to have. My attempts to remain polite were one repetition of "no, you only ordered one" from giving way to the version of me that gets people fired (you'll read about that version of me in the Tech Hotel story).

The only reason that didn't happen was because a manager finally stepped in to find out what was taking so long. It took her less than a minute to find the source of the confusion: he'd been trying to give me someone else's order the whole time. He could have discovered that himself if only he'd listened to me instead of arguing.

Not every bad situation can be placed on the heads of the customer rather than the employees. At the same time, far too many people expect the person behind the register to reset corporate policy or cheat the laws of physics.

In one of the milder conflicts I handled, a man phoned to ask my coworker if we had a particular item in stock. We did at that time, but what my coworker didn't know was that I was moments away from selling the last one. Even if my coworker had taken the initiative to put the item on hold, despite the customer not asking him to, I probably would've sold the thing before he'd completed the process.

When the customer came in, he was rather irate that we didn't have his item. I did everything I could to make it right. I found another one in stock at a store not far away and called to make sure it would be waiting on the customer when he arrived. He still wasn't happy, but he didn't feel the need to cuss us out or threaten us, which puts him ahead of a lot of other people.

The way I look at it is this: even if you can make a valid case that we made a mistake, the mistake is still made. We can't get the item back from the other customer or light candles in a circle to conjure up a new one out of thin air.

All I ever expect out of customer service employees is exactly what we did for him: find the best reasonable solution possible. More times than not, a little patience and understanding has been far more rewarding than getting irate: extra fries when I didn't pitch a fit about them having trouble with a register, an extra dessert for being understanding about a mistake with my order. People are willing to reward that behavior because they appreciate it that much. I once had a man tell me that throughout an entire day, I was the one and only person to say a kind word to him. I didn't even think I'd been particularly nice to him and yet, it was enough for him to comment on it and thank me. Knowing that small amount of decency was enough to make a big impression on someone keeps me more mindful than ever about how I act.

More than any other reason I can recall, us not having something in stock would send people into a rage. One man reported me to our corporate office, requiring me to explain my actions to them. My sin? Telling him that we didn't carry the record needle he was looking for, but that if he could give me the make and model of his player I would most likely be able to special order it for him.

If I was working at Taco Bell and we didn't have tacos to sell, maybe I could understand a customer getting upset. Record needles though? We had a parts catalog with a section of different needles covering several pages. I couldn't believe how many different ones existed. In my two years at the store, I can count on one hand the number we sold, and it was never the same one twice.

Even if we were selling them on a regular basis, we were a small store and didn't have the shelf space needed to stock so many different types (we didn't stock turntables, either...not even the ones that were our brand). The customer found this offensive. He was furious that we didn't keep his particular needle in the store. He demanded my name, telling me that he intended to report me. When I gave it to him, he demanded my last name as well. The guy was so unhinged over such a minor inconvenience that I was legitimately afraid for him to have my first and last name. I staunchly refused to give him my last name no matter how loudly he demanded it. I was glad that the interaction was taking place over the phone so that he didn't know what I looked like. I told him that I was the only Chad working for the company in this area and assured him they'd know who he meant.

I'll never understand why us not having a record needle readily available on the shelf of our little store was enough cause to not only yell at an employee who had no say in such a decision, but also try to get him in trouble over it. Corporate, after hearing my account of what occurred, immediately dropped the matter. I give them credit for not taking the customer's side, which I believe some companies would do no matter how ridiculous the complaint.

I've said how the company didn't put any extreme expectations on us as far as sales went. "Upsell X times a day or get fired!" "Sign up Y percent of your customers for our reward card or be written up!" I don't think I could work in that kind of environment. But we did implement a policy that almost caused a fight. And by fight, I mean a genuine physical altercation.

Corporate wanted us to refrain from using any negative language. How do you tell someone, "No, we don't have that in stock" without using "negative" language? Even when that's followed with a solution: "I can order it" or "We'll have more delivered on Tuesday" or even "I can see if the store down the road has one." All of that is dependent on the context of "there are none currently present in this store."

If I don't understand what it is you're wanting from me, no amount of my willingness to comply matters. When I was in school, maybe fourth or fifth grade, my teacher got fed up with the class being loud. When the bell rang, she told us to tiptoe out. I thought I understood what she meant: be quiet.

Being as silent as I possibly could, without a single word spoken and even being careful not to bump anything, I picked up my books and walked to the door. The teacher called me back. "I said tiptoe," she said. She enunciated "tiptoe" like it was two words with caps lock turned on and a period after each syllable. So, this time I took her literally. I stood up on my toes and did a John Cleese-esque high step placing each foot carefully and deliberately. "Oh, just get out of here," she grumbled.

I was not being a smart alec; I just didn't (and still don't) understand exactly what she was expecting out of me. I did the best I could with what I understood to be the expectation. I was the only one to be called back, so I can only assume that I was the only one who didn't get it. I'm not aware of any of my classmates from that time being on the autism spectrum, which makes me wonder about the correlation.

Similarly with this whole push to not use negative language, I never saw any of my coworkers struggle with it the way I did. Did I take it too literally? Did I take it too far? I really can't tell you. All I can say for sure is that the initiative turned the poor salesman in me into a terrible one.

A man probably in his mid-twenties entered the store with two of his friends. The guy in question was a fairly large man but not threatening at first. I'd even say that he was pleasant when he walked in looking for a capacitor or a resistor or some other small part which we usually had in stock. But not today.

While stumbling all over myself trying to offer a solution without using any negative language, I attempted to let him know that I could help him find an alternative or could get one for him at a later date. I think he was getting frustrated with me not being straightforward about us not having the part in stock, and looking back on it I can't say I blame him. A clear "no" is so much better than a convoluted "let me show you what else we have instead." I don't want to know what else you have; I want to know if you have what I'm looking for.

Unfortunately for us all, I didn't recognize his growing frustration until it was full blown rage. It was the only time in my retail career that I had someone threaten to "come across that counter" to beat me up (his actual language was a bit more PG-13). He dared me to call the police, which I might've done except that I didn't want to take my eyes off the guy in case he decided to make a move.

Even though he was larger than me, I was still practicing my Karate enough that I occasionally gave private lessons to people. I was afraid to get into a fight because of what it might mean for my continued employment, not to mention my odds of winning if the fight became three on one, but I was also sizing up my options depending on whether he decided to lean over the counter to grab me or leap over it. In either case, I could use his size and momentum against him if I was smart about it. So, in another moment that might have gotten me in trouble if anyone had been around to hear me, I looked him right in the eye and told him to "bring it on."

Thankfully, his two friends were less hot headed. They calmed their buddy down, apologized profusely, and ushered him out the door. I don't know if he would've made good on his threat, but it's better for all of us that he didn't.

I would say the "no negative language" campaign backfired spectacularly, at least as far as I was concerned. Obviously the simple, clear "no, but here's a solution" didn't work out too well with Record Needle Guy, but "I want your name because I'm reporting you to corporate" is a lot less nerve-wracking than "I'm going to come across this counter and kick your butt!"

After this incident, I quit trying to perform those verbal gymnastics. I talked like I knew how to talk – with that little bit of salesmanship that had allowed our little store to sell more computers than the larger ones in the district for at least one quarter. Either nobody noticed or nobody cared, because no word was ever spoken to me about it.

Not all of my stories from my time at this store involve customers. We had some strange internal drama that resulted in a lot of staff turnover, including three managers. One of those managers was caught "borrowing" money from the register. I came in for my shift to discover she'd been fired earlier that day; the district manager told me what was happening. He was there leading a surprise inventory of the whole store - making sure that we weren't missing anything other than the money he knew about.

When midnight came, I decided I had to leave. I wanted to do my part as a good employee, especially because I was glad they hadn't decided to fire everyone else along with her (something that'd happened before with me being the only survivor), but after being in classes all day I was exhausted. As 1:00 A.M. loomed, I nervously approached the district manager to tell him that I had school in the morning and couldn't stay any longer. To my relief, he gave me a pat on the back for my hard work and sent me home.

By the time I got back to my apartment I was so tired that I was evidently weaving side to side with my car. It wasn't enough to be a danger (I never crossed out of my lane) but it was enough to get me pulled over on the suspicion of drunk driving. Again, to my surprise, the cop let me go without much hassle, so I was able to get to bed soon after.

I felt bad for that manager because she was a nice person, even if she wasn't the best at her job. I wanted to believe that she really was just borrowing the money with the intention of paying it back, but if it'd been a one-time thing she probably wouldn't have gotten caught. She wasn't the first nice person at this place to bring negative consequences upon herself. As much as I hated seeing bad things happen to people I liked, it did teach me a life lesson: being nice is not the only quality someone needs to be successful.

The Borrowing Manager was the last of the three to be fired from that same store in less than two years. To tell you what happened to the other two, I need to take you back in time.

When I first started working for the company, I was hired by a store near my college campus. A few months after I started, I was told that a small downtown store was being revamped in an attempt to improve sales there. I was familiar with the area because all of us college kids hung out at a mall nearby, but I'd never been to that shopping plaza so I can't say what state the store or staff were in before I got there. However, I learned that the store wasn't simply bringing in new help for the existing staff - every single person at that location had been fired. I was joining a brand-new staff. Most, if not all of them, had been with the company longer than I had, but none of us had ever worked at that location before.

I don't know why I was selected - maybe it's because I was good with technology and deemed a potential asset, or maybe it was just because I was the new kid and easy to move around. Whatever the reason, I was sent to the new store along with another full-time employee, a part-timer, and a manager who was also a long-haired guitarist for a rock'n'roll cover band.

I'll call the manager James because my wife and I are watching *Lost* (she's never seen it!) and that was just revealed as Sawyer's real name. James' favorite musician was Alice Cooper. Being a fan myself (I even have a personally autographed album cover framed on my wall), we hit it off immediately. We'd talk about music, and, if we had no customers in the store, would listen to the local rock radio station while we worked.

I was quickly designated the only person to make coffee whenever I was scheduled to work. James would tell me my coffee was so good that if I were a woman, he'd marry me. He was full of humorous quips like that which still come to mind on occasion, most of them too R-rated to repeat here. One of his favorites was a much cruder version of "if it was up your butt, you'd know where it was!" He liked to tell me about his girlfriend, who was significantly younger than he was. I thought it was odd but never judged him, which is probably a good thing since I myself ended up marrying a woman much younger than I am. I tell you all that to illustrate how well he and I got along. I considered him a friend as well as my boss.

More than that, he was a mentor. James was the main reason I was able to weather the chaos that hit that store in the coming months. He was the first one to give me the keys to the front door, teach me how to open and close, and entrust me with making bank runs. I became his right-hand man, which gave me the knowledge and experience I needed to stand strong when the need arose. I like to think he would've been proud to see me do well in his absence.

I've wondered at times if I could have prevented his demise within the company. Was being gone when the hammer fell the only thing that saved me, or could I have held back the hammer if I'd been there to help? But I'm getting ahead of myself; let me back up for a moment...

Our part-timer left to give birth and never returned, which was too bad because everyone liked her. She was smart and sweet. She also added a woman's perspective to an otherwise all male staff, which we missed long after she was gone. She's the only person I can remember who decided to leave rather than being told to, until I resigned nearly two years later. The entire staff aside from me was fired at least twice (if you count those that James and I replaced), a phenomenon I've never experienced before or since, along with smaller-scale shake-ups like the Borrowing Manager. I started wondering if there was a curse on that location.

That ominous air of extensive turnover was still in my future when I worked under James. I expected nothing but good times. We had a laid-back atmosphere, fun conversations, pranks, and, at least as far as I could tell at the time, an increasingly good reputation in our area. James once hooked me up with a turntable someone had brought in for repair and then never picked up. He said it was either give it to me or throw it out.

That sort of thing actually happened frequently: people would bring in something to get fixed, we'd send it to our repair center, get it back, and then be unable to get in touch with the owner. As I've said, we were a small store; we didn't have the physical space available to keep unclaimed repairs indefinitely, so after calling the owners repeatedly for months, James would sell the items under the counter (instead of trashing them according to company policy). Then, whenever he'd made enough money to do so, he'd treat us all to pizza. None of the other managers ever did that for us.

When we were certain she wouldn't be returning, we replaced our lost part-timer with a new hire. He was so bad at his job that James told me several times he should fire the guy. The problem was the kid was so nice that James didn't have the heart to get rid of him. I think he would've had to eventually, but that decision was soon taken out of his hands.

Other than James' predicament with the new kid, life was good at our store. I expected to work with James and the other full-timer until I graduated, then visit them whenever I came back into town. Life was about to show me how unpredictable reality can be.

I had a weekend off, which I was spending with my

parents. I wasn't just off work; I was hours away for the entire weekend. Since personal cell phones were the exception rather than the rule at that time, I was, for all practical purposes, unreachable.

I returned to my apartment Sunday night, went to class Monday morning, and then went to work for my regularly scheduled shift. When I walked into the store, I saw a woman I didn't recognize. This was nothing unusual, as we would sometimes call in help from other stores if one of our regulars got sick. With me out of touch all weekend, we would've been short-staffed if even one of the other guys couldn't work. So, I thought nothing of an unrecognizable face behind the counter. I just wondered who was sick and hoped nothing was being passed around.

I headed to the office to put my stuff down and get ready for my shift. "Can I help you?" she asked as I stepped from the sales floor into the back hallway.

"I work here," I replied.

"Then there's something you need to know," she said. She proceeded to tell me how every single employee of the store except for me had been fired while I was gone. She, the new manager (the same one who would soon be fired for "borrowing" money), and I were now the only employees. Of course, that didn't last long, but neither did she or the new employee. She either didn't know the details behind the decision to fire everyone or didn't want to tell me. I heard rumors that it had to do with missing money and/or inventory, but that was all I knew for several weeks. I didn't have a way to contact James or anyone else directly.

I was glad to eventually have the opportunity to talk to my former coworker about what had happened. Everything I know comes from his account. I can neither verify nor disprove any of it, other than offering the most circumstantial of evidence and my personal belief that neither of these men were dishonest.

The first thing that James drilled into my head when training me to do bank runs was to always, always, always check the receipt. The cash from the day's sales had to be deposited and the numbers logged into our corporate database. If the numbers on the receipt didn't match what our bank slip said, I was to demand it be corrected immediately. I would assume that a bank of all places could be trusted to get their number right, but you've heard the saying about what happens when you assume, haven't you?

The number of times the bank got our deposit amount wrong made me wonder why we continued to do business with them. I don't know how many times James had to have his deposits corrected; he made the bank run far more frequently than I did, but if my memory is accurate as many as a quarter of mine were wrong. Most of the time, the differences were a matter of a few dollars. Occasionally, though, they'd amount to hundreds or even thousands of dollars missing. The weekend I was away was one of those times.

As much as I hate to lay this on the shoulders of my coworker (because if he told the truth, the fault actually lies with the bank), James should never have trusted him to make the bank run. When James was training me, he would always double-check my numbers. It was a good thing, too, because I missed a discrepancy on the receipt during one of my first runs. If James hadn't checked it, I might have been the one getting fired for missing money. I learned my lesson and it never happened again on my watch.

That's exactly what I think happened while I was gone. James, having become accustomed to not needing to double-check my receipts, either failed to do so with my coworker or didn't look closely enough. The discrepancy immediately caught the eye of someone high up the chain, who then swooped in for a lightning-fast investigation and mass firing.

If James had been able to convince the higher-ups that the bank had made a mistake, a problem with our inventory still would've raised questions and may have been what sealed his fate. Part of the investigation of the bank numbers included a full inventory of the store, and it didn't go well.

To prevent the loss of some of our more expensive items, we kept a display model on the shelves while storing the sealed boxes in the back. A number of those boxes turned out to be empty. I don't know exactly what was missing, but if I were to use low estimates with minimal losses, I'd still calculate no less than a few hundred dollars missing from the bank deposit plus a few hundred more in missing inventory.

I can only guess at what happened to the missing items, but I do have a plausible theory. We periodically inventoried everything in the store. Yet even when doing a thorough count, we didn't necessarily check the contents of the boxes. We would've seen the boxes we expected to see, verified that the item numbers matched what the system said we had, and moved on without ever checking the contents of packages which shouldn't have ever been opened. We might not have known about any problems unless we'd sold one of the empty boxes.

That means it's entirely possible that those boxes were empty before any of us ever set foot in that store. I figure that the previous staff wasn't fired without a reason. If they'd been dishonest, might one of them have helped him or herself to some free electronics before leaving? Was that inventory missing before we arrived and we never noticed? If that wasn't the case, then the other most plausible answer is that James took them. I prefer to believe the former scenario.

Even if James had been crooked, I can't believe he'd be dumb enough to be caught so easily. One missing item or even a few spread out across a variety of different categories might've earned him the disapproval of Corporate without costing him his job. An entire selection of the same item is much easier to notice and far more suspicious.

No matter who was at fault for the missing inventory, James' luck was epically bad to have the bank error call such scrutiny down upon the store before we could discover and handle the discrepancy ourselves.

Whatever the truth may be, it cost James and my coworker their jobs. The new kid was destined to be fired one way or another, Corporate simply did what James didn't have the heart to. That left me as the sole employee left standing because I was the only one who pulled my weight and wasn't caught up in the scandal.

Working in familiar surroundings with all new faces was weird. I felt as if I'd walked out of one store and into a different one without realizing it - one that looked exactly the same except for the people. The new manager didn't express the same confidence in me that James had. I didn't judge her too harshly because she didn't know me, but I began feeling like she relied on me because she had no other options rather than because she felt I could handle myself. Of course, knowing what I do now, it's entirely possible that she wanted everyone at arm's length so that nobody would notice her "borrowing" money.

Even though I never thought as highly of her as I did James, nor did I learn anything new from her (the brevity of her employment didn't give us a lot of time together), I got along well enough with both her and the person who filled her shoes after she left. Yet, there was always a disconnect between them and me. James was the only one of my four managers (counting the one at the original store from which I was transferred) who didn't treat me like a child.

I try not to blame them too much because they weren't the only ones. I was a college kid who looked so much younger than my years that I got carded when I went to the theater to see *Resident Evil,* an R-rated zombie movie. I also got scrutinized a few times for suspicion of underage drinking, even when I was of legal age and had no interest in touching a drop of alcohol. I've been pulled over because the officer thought I looked too young to have a license and was scrutinized multiple times by the same person at video rental stores when I wanted to check out horror movies ("I need to see your ID again before I let you rent these"). I was used to being seen as a child. But it was hard going back to that mindset after James had treated me like an adult.

I think my quiet demeanor contributed to the perceptions of me. Had I been more assertive, more demanding, or maybe just more confident perhaps I could've made myself harder to overlook or dismiss. When I was accused of playing games on company time when I was fixing a problem a customer had caused with our display computer, I didn't defend myself. When my responsibilities were reset to the default of any standard sales associate, I didn't make a case for the additional duties I was able to perform. I guess I thought that the other managers would see for themselves what I could do, just as James had, and decide to once again entrust me with more responsibility. For one reason or another, that never happened.

Whatever my bosses thought of me, I was the only

constant at that store for nearly two years. I was well versed in all the duties the managers performed aside from handling the employees. I considered telling Corporate that if they were going to keep firing the managers, they might as well let me run the place. If I hadn't wanted to get a job in broadcasting as soon as possible after graduating, I might've done that.

After I graduated, I left the company on good terms never expecting to return but with no reason to burn any bridges. I didn't have the connections I thought I would've because I had so little time to get to know that last manager, nor did I ever return to that town as frequently as I hoped I would. If nothing else though, I wanted to be able to call on them for references.

As I moved around in the upcoming years, there were times I considered going to a local store to see if they would hire me, but I never could bring myself to return to the world of retail after leaving it. Even if I'd liked that kind of work more than I did, I was afraid that if I got hired everyone else would somehow end up fired a few months later.

5

No Ragerts

My favorite tattoo blunder that I see online every so often is "NO RAGERTS." There are a few variations on that, but "ragerts" is my favorite because it's fun to say. If I could call any aspect of my working life a regret, it would be that I never followed through with my dream of working in broadcasting. I suppose I don't have any true regrets because if my path had been different, maybe I wouldn't be where I am now. Be that as it may, I put a significant amount of effort into an exciting career that didn't pan out.

With my heart full of aspirations, I left WDVI to become a professional DJ. Nothing was more important to me than making sure I had my own radio show on my college's campus station, WRAM, as soon as possible. I was on the air no less than twice a week for the rest of my time at that school if class was in session, and sometimes when it wasn't.

When my second year rolled around, I was given the keys to the kingdom: I became the student manager of the station. That didn't mean I could do whatever I wanted, but it did give me freedom I'd never had before. I took advantage of my position to test the boundaries of what was acceptable. It was my opportunity to play the kinds of heavy metal music most stations wouldn't allow.

I faced some of the same criticisms at WRAM that I had at WDVI, although the context was a little different. Rock music was fine here; nobody took issue if I wanted to play that Petra song "I Love the Lord." That sort of music was not only acceptable but popular around this Christian college (except that it was out of date - Petra was old, bands like Jars of Clay were the newest, greatest thing). Some of my other music, though, raised a few eyebrows.

When I say I played metal I'm not talking only about the glam styles of bands like Def Leppard or Poison, although I certainly included that sort of thing (except that being a Christian school I would have been playing Stryper and Holy Soldier). I wanted to subject the world to sounds like those of Slayer and Pantera (in the Christian music world that would be Living Sacrifice and Tourniquet). No radio station I knew was going to air music that heavy, even less so the Christian market stations, but since I was managing WRAM I decided I would play it until someone told me I couldn't. Nobody ever did. That is to say, nobody who could stop me ever did.

My staunchest challenge came from a fellow student. I don't remember his name because I never knew him outside of scheduling the time slot for his show and making sure he was behaving while on the air. What I do remember about him is that he took his responsibilities as a DJ seriously. That was a good thing; he did good work that gained my respect. He was also fully mainstream. He didn't like the edgy music I was playing and said so to me. He thought we should be limiting our music to the more popular mainstream bands, what we called "CHR" (Christian Hit Radio) and "AC" (Adult Contemporary) in those days. Heavy metal wasn't appropriate for Christian radio in his view.

He had no authority over me, but his criticism was presented respectfully and was reasonable enough that I felt like I should justify myself. I didn't want to have the attitude "I do what I want, and nobody can tell me otherwise." Besides, if he objected strongly enough, he could go over my head and try to have me removed from the station if he chose to. As far as I know, he never attempted to do that, but having a reasoned response to his criticism seemed wise in case I had to repeat it to someone who did have authority.

My reasoning, which I still stand behind, was that every Christian radio station in the nation was playing the mainstream hit songs. If we, a small college station with limited reach and

DJ talent who were students still learning their skills, were playing nothing but the same music that listeners could hear on the professional stations around town, why should they listen to us? That didn't mean we shouldn't play some of that music (Jars of Clay was and still is my favorite mainstream Christian band of that era and I certainly wanted to support them), but I felt that we should offer sounds that listeners couldn't find elsewhere. If any other radio station in the entire state of Alabama was playing songs by Deliverance, I wasn't aware of it.

I can't say that my way of thinking made me a hit - I had listeners, but I wasn't necessarily popular. I tried my best to become known as the go-to DJ of Christian metal in my area, but the limited reach of the station kept me from being able to attract much attention.

That's not to say that everyone ignored me or the other DJs that helped promote the station. Mainstream Christian artists like Bob Carlisle and members of Audio Adrenaline recorded station ID spots for us. Metal musicians like Scott Wenzel from Whitecross recorded interviews with me. Peter King, host of MTV's "Sandblast" and lead guitarist for Dakoda Motor Co, even recorded a spot that mentioned me by name, which I used in pretty much every show I ever had from that point forward. The highlight of my efforts was getting to interview Ben Huggins, a member of my favorite band: Galactic Cowboys.

My radio station position gave me access to musicians that I wouldn't have had otherwise and a reason to record our conversations. These people were appreciative that I was playing their music and happy to lend their names to the effort of drawing more listeners. But I wanted more attention from record labels and magazines. With so few shows on the air playing metal music in my region, I continued to hope that someone would see me as an opportunity to reach a larger audience, which I could then use to strengthen my appeal as a DJ to the point where I could convince a larger station to want me as their metal voice. I wanted to be the bridge between the music makers and the ones who could air that music.

I mentioned earlier the tendency for auties to become hyper focused. Whether that affected my choices or if I would've done everything the same way if autism had played no part is more than I can say. What I do know, thanks to hindsight, is that my focus on the campus station kept me from developing relationships with the local commercial stations. I felt like time spent elsewhere was time I could be putting into making WRAM successful. I already had increasing demands on my time thanks to working at the electronics store when I wasn't in class. How could I fit working for another radio station into that schedule?

In an attempt to find something more in my field, I picked up a weekend job as a club DJ. Because it was late at night, it never conflicted with anything else I was doing. I even got hired by a second club (which I declined after finding out that my first gig there would be ladies' night with a team of male strippers as the main event). I soon realized that while being a club DJ was a fun way to make some extra money, it wasn't a viable career path if I wasn't willing to embrace a wild party lifestyle.

I wanted WRAM to be a success, and I was having fun with it. I've kept up with many of my favorite promotional spots and revisit them from time to time. Far from the hokey efforts of a goofy kid, I'm still proud of them so I like to think I was doing some good work there.

Fun though it was, I can honestly say that enjoyment wasn't my only focus. I was looking to the future. I thought that graduating with managerial experience and a production reel of promos and commercials would look good on a resume. I thought it'd be my years of experience that would be pivotal in finding a job; I didn't understand that who you know is as important, if not more so, than what you know. I had very few connections when I graduated.

Only once did I come close to having my dedication to WRAM work in my favor. I was offered the opportunity to manage WDVI, the station that started me on this road of broadcasting. When the owner decided that he didn't just want to hire a manager but wanted to get away from the station entirely, I faced a bigger decision than just taking a job. The station was mine if I wanted it, but I had to be able to buy it. The owner gave me a deadline to make my decision. If I decided not to take it, he would offer it to someone else.

I spoke to investors, but I wasn't salesman enough to get

anyone interested. I didn't know who to talk to or how to approach them. I had no business plan - what did I know about running a business? I could run the technical side of a radio station; beyond that I was lost without anyone beside me who could fill in where I was deficient.

When I was done making my sales pitches, I had raised a grand total (including the money that I myself had to put towards the purchase) of $0.

As far as I know, my managerial experience never affected any other job I ever got. Nobody ever expressed any interest in it. Maybe that's because the next few years were a muddled mess for me.

To add insult to injury, I heard that the campus station shut down shortly after I graduated. I have amazing memories and I did learn some skills that continue to be useful, so I don't feel like my time there was a total waste. Even so, I feel like neither I or the university got much return out of the four years of focused dedication I poured into that station.

NO RAGERTS? At that time, I still thought bigger and better things awaited me in the world of broadcasting. My first job out of college was working for a TV station, which filled me with confidence. Certainly, there was nothing to regret yet.

6

TV Toner

I knew that when I graduated, the campus station would no longer be available to me, and I never intended to make a lifelong career out of my electronics retail job. This meant I had to figure out what to do next. I didn't really want to move away from the area I lived in, what we called "L.A." (Lower Alabama), but before I had any success finding a job there, I was approached with an offer to work with a UPN affiliated TV station back in my hometown. Does anyone even remember that network anymore? I jumped at the chance, perhaps too eagerly given the way things worked out, to have a job in my field immediately after graduation, and at a network station no less. I thought I was on track for a successful career in broadcasting. If I'd only known...

My time at the TV station was a mixed bag of exciting experiences and troubling disappointments. To start with, the job wasn't at all what I expected to be doing as a professional with a degree and roughly six years of experience producing, editing, and performing not to mention my three years of managing. I did none of that at my new job. I spent the vast majority of my time at UPN performing the tedious task of marking tapes. What does that mean? Grab an aspirin, because I'm about to explain in more detail than any reasonable human being would wish for.

As a local station, we featured a certain amount of locally produced content. (I'll talk more about that later.) As a UPN affiliate, we aired a certain amount of what UPN told us to - the programs that aired on all of their stations. We had a variety of shows with a focus on younger audiences. One of the most popular that I can recall was "Sweet Valley High," a "Saved by the Bell" style comedy about twin girls in high school. There was a run of "extreme" cartoons like "Extreme Dinosaurs" which I barely remember outside of a team of anthropomorphic dinosaurs fighting bad guys (not unlike "Teenage Mutant Ninja Turtles"), and "Extreme Ghostbusters" which I enjoyed so much I now own three different copies and have chased down autographs from some of the stars. That one was a continuation of the more popular "Real Ghostbusters" series with both tied into the movie universe created by Dan Ackroyd and Harold Ramis.

All of those shows (and many more) we taped off a UPN

satellite feed. Each episode included a certain number of national commercials that would play on every UPN station around the country. Either before or after that was a limited amount of blank space for any local commercials that affiliates wanted to include. The amount of time for each commercial break, national and local combined, was set by UPN so any ads we ran had to fit within the slot they gave us.

How do you get local ads mixed in with the national ones? That's where I came in. Editing the commercials into the feed would have been possible but impractical. Multiple shows with multiple breaks each? That takes too much time, especially considering that the ads weren't always the same. We had a machine that would automatically play the current ads at the appropriate times. The way the machine knew when to start playing and when to stop so that the show could resume was by way of tones that had to be inserted by us at the station. I'm sure you can guess whose job it was to insert those tones.

That was the vast majority of my job day in and day out: load the latest episode of a show into a specialized tape deck, scan forward to find where the local commercial time slot began, drop a tone, scan to the end of the slot to drop another tone, find the next time slot, and the next until I reached the end of the episode, then rinse and repeat for the next show. It was mind-numbingly dull work.

I wanted to be creative - produce commercial spots, run some equipment, host a show. My WDVI commercials were still being used, and I was proud of the ones I'd produced for WRAM, so I had confidence in my ability to do good work. My heart wasn't in the marking of tapes all day every day. It felt like grunt work that didn't require a college degree. My supervisor had to keep me on task when I got distracted. I might have been a little more enthusiastic if I'd been making more money, but my paycheck was another rude awakening in the real world after college.

I tried to focus on the rare opportunities I had to go beyond my regular duties. The most exciting of those was the chance to work on a live local TV show we produced in our own studio. It wasn't anything glamorous; I mostly just aided the director - the equivalent of a stagehand. Even so, it was a break from marking tapes with experience that I hoped would eventually prove useful in advancing my broadcasting career.

My last day working for the station, I was asked to be a guest on the show. The host interviewed me with questions about my time at UPN and what my future held. I wish I'd had more time to prepare for the interview; being invited on as a guest was a surprise, so I feel like I came across with a presentation of "golly gee willikers, look at me, I'm on the TV box," but I enjoyed the attention.

That was actually my second time on the show. The first was on Halloween. Back in high school, I used to create odd home movies with my buddy Johnny Dobbs and some of our other friends. We created the character of Spatula-Man, played by me. Over the years, I worked on the character's costume to create a faceless ghoul in a robe wearing a longhaired rockstar wig. I also wore a Santa hat because my alias was The Evil Meatcleaver-Santa Twin, a name you have to see the movie to understand.

As Halloween approached, I told one of the hosts and the director of our live TV program about an idea I had. Nobody else knew about it. Early Halloween morning before anyone else arrived, I donned my Spatula-Man costume and hid in the shadows of an unused set in the studio. At a predetermined point in the show, I slowly rose from my hiding place, a black-clad figure in a Santa hat appearing out of nowhere. The cameras only saw the hosts' shocked reactions until they called me over so that the viewing audience could get a look at me. The host that was expecting it played his part perfectly, not letting on that he knew anything about me. The host that didn't know what was happening was the real entertainment for the viewing audience. His bewilderment provided us and the audience with entertainment we'd be laughing about for weeks.

Then something happened that I didn't expect. The hosts wanted me to join the program! I had to improvise, as I was expecting to scare everyone then walk off the set. My Spatula-Man persona was a hokey homemade movie villain that I'd turned into a creepy, if bizarre, but mostly silent figure. I didn't have a TV personality prepared. My mind whirled as I tried to figure out how to be creepy but charming with an *Addams*

Family kind of vibe.

My anxiety deepened when I had to read. This being a local show, part of the reason people tuned in was to hear the hosts wish viewers happy birthday or anniversary as requests were called in. The director or stagehand (usually me when I was there, but of course I was on set today) would bring the list of names to the hosts, handing the paper through the window of the set (the set being the front porch of a house). The hosts wanted me to be the one to read the latest list except that I couldn't see through the mask that hid my face! I struggled to read all the names while trying to maintain an air that was more creepy than bumbling. I'm not entirely sure I succeeded, but I did get through it.

I can't say that Spatula-Man was a smash hit. Nobody ever chased me down for a return appearance or sought out autographs. I doubt there are more than a handful of people who remember it at all - maybe not even that many. Still, it was fun, and there's a certain amount of satisfaction in knowing that my character appeared on public TV, no matter how small the audience might have been.

To this day, I'm not sure that anyone but the one host and maybe the director ever knew it was me under the mask. When I left the station people were still asking the question "Who was that masked character?" while the few people who knew feigned ignorance.

My time at the station came to an end when a family

friend told me that her church wanted to hire a full-time youth pastor for the first time. Knowing my history with church involvement and my knowledge of the Bible, she wanted me to consider the job. Thanks to my dissatisfaction with my job at the TV station, I decided to give it a shot. This wasn't my wisest decision.

I don't think knowing about my autism would've mattered for my job with UPN. I didn't mind the isolation of my tasks, although I didn't realize how well-suited I am for something like that compared to the average person. The dull repetition of what I did every day would surely have bored any intelligent, creative person. If I'd been more outgoing and assertive, maybe I could've pushed for opportunities to do more of what drew me to broadcasting in the first place, and if I could've done that I most likely would've stayed longer. I was too quick to abandon my career path in my search for something more fulfilling. Depending on how you want to look at it, that was either the best decision I could have made or the worst. Certainly, I would've never expected the next few years of my life to go as badly as they did.

7

Youth Pastor Disaster

What on earth made me think I would be a good youth minister for a church? All I can say is that I was young, I was blinded by my career in broadcasting not turning out like I wanted, and I wanted to serve God. Was I following what God wanted me to do, or did I make a wrong turn because I didn't take enough time to consider the insanity of my decision? Even now, I can't say for sure. My failures at the church taught me a lot and put me on the path that brought me to Georgia, which was the first step in all the crazy choices that got me to where I am now. Does that mean God wanted me to learn those lessons, directing me towards failures that would redirect my path to what He wanted it to be, or does it mean that He brought something good out of my bad decisions? I can envision Him with His hand up to His head as he says, "Oh, Chad, you don't know what you're getting yourself into. It's a good thing for you I can fix this."

What I do know is that one way or another, this was not a job that was going to last long. On the one hand, I was not a good youth leader. I had little patience with the kids when they didn't listen to me, and the problems I ran into were way over my head. On the other hand, unrealistic demands were placed upon me. It's entirely possible that even a good youth minister would have struggled here.

I stepped into a difficult situation from the get-go. A friend of the kids had committed suicide recently, and they were hurting. If I did anything good at that church, I think I was able to help them through that difficult time. At least I hope so. As someone who suffered from severe depression for many years myself, I'd wondered if I might ever get to the point of suicide and had thought a lot about the spiritual consequences. When facing questions from those affected by it, I had answers both from my own personal contemplation and from my study of the Bible.

I hadn't been in the job more than a couple of weeks before these teens were asking me questions like whether their friend was in Hell because she'd taken her own life. I wouldn't wish a start like that on any youth minister, even a good one. Looking back on it now, I realize that my answers were philosophical and academic, but I had an opportunity to connect with these kids on an emotional level that's beyond what I'm usually able to do, certainly with people I don't know.

The kids were not all gloom and doom, though. We had some good times together. The first of those was the result of fortunate timing and my desire to make use of the influence and connections of my radio days.

I've always been a supporter of *HM Magazine* (originally called *Heaven's Metal*), which was the go-to publication for metal music for Christians. I became friends with founder and original editor Doug Van Pelt and even went on to do some freelance writing for the magazine under Doug's successor.

Doug started an outreach campaign as part of a prison ministry. I was already planning to participate myself, so I thought it would be a good opportunity to get the youth group involved. It was a chance to show them something of who I was and see how they responded.

This was an opportunity for us to interact, by way of letters, with people who had made decisions bad enough to put them behind bars and see the impact that Jesus Christ had on their lives. Some of these men were finding hope for the first time and willing to talk about it. I wanted my influence to be more than a list of what to do and what to avoid; I wanted to delve into more profound consequences and impact of faith. I saw this campaign as a way to get that conversation started.

Doug provided incentives by way of random drawings

for prizes, like music compilations the magazine produced and albums donated by some of the artists he knew. Because we had multiple people participating, we won a few of those drawings. I don't think the kids were as excited about it as I was but I was proud of their efforts, so it made me feel good to give them some recognition and hand out their prizes.

I have to admit that I thought my metalhead background would make me look cool in the eyes of the younger generation. I could almost guarantee that no other youth minister from that little town had ever been in a mosh pit or hosted a radio show that didn't consider any song too heavy to play. I quickly learned through Doug's campaign that I was dealing almost entirely with pop and country fans, not rockers. They weren't excited because it wasn't their style.

I tried a few more attempts at using my style of music to teach them lessons, but it never had the effect I was hoping for. If anyone was telling someone to turn their music down it was probably going to be them saying it to me! Here I was the adult head of the youth group and somehow, in some ways, I was the one who fit in the least.

That's not to say that the kids and I didn't get along. I knew more about the state of technology, the world of video games, and details of the latest movies than anyone else at the church did. Maybe we couldn't connect through music, but we had plenty of other shared interests we could discuss. It was enough to keep me hopeful for a while.

Trouble started brewing when the high school group's attendance began dropping. I was trying everything I could think of, but part of the problem was out of my control. Some of the older students were graduating and moving off to college. My best friends at church when I was growing up were in the same graduating class as I was, so we all left for college at the same time. If they'd gone first and left me behind. maybe I would've been less motivated to stay involved with my youth group. That's exactly what was happening here. The church wasn't a large one, so if two students graduated and two others stopped coming because their friends weren't there any longer, that was a significant percentage of the group gone.

If that wasn't enough, we didn't have a college level program at all. I had no idea if it was better to create a new one or try to keep the graduating seniors involved with the current group. Considering how few of them I had and how strong their connections were to their younger classmates, I opted for the latter. But how to create events that appealed to both the high schoolers and the college students who wouldn't always be in town to attend was a challenge I was ill-prepared to face.

While I was scratching my head over different possibilities and talking to other youth ministers about what they would do in my situation, some of the parents confronted me about the low attendance. I told them about events I was planning to reinvigorate interest, particularly among the college students. I was hoping to stir up some excitement and maybe get some ideas I hadn't considered or even some offers to help. What I got was the exact opposite.

Every single date I attempted to plan was on a weekend that one or more of the youth group was going to miss because of a ball game or family trip out of town. When I asked for input on better dates for future planning I was told, if not in so many words, that it was my job to figure it out. How was I supposed to improve attendance when so many of the families already had other things to do?

I tried relying more heavily on our Wednesday night Bible studies. Growing up in a Baptist church, my friends and I loved Wednesday nights. The church would feed us, after which we'd play pool or ping pong for a while before having a group study that lasted thirty minutes or so. I tried doing the same thing here.

That went well until the seniors started getting ready for graduation. When I would ask about them coming, I was told a number of times that they got busy and forgot. I get that. As an adult, I attend a regular Tuesday night gathering at my church. Even among responsible adults who want to be there, I see all the time how easy it is to forget what day it is or to get so involved with something that time slips away. We all need reminders sometimes.

If we'd had cell phones like we do now, I could've called or sent text messages reminding everyone to come. But I didn't have that option, and calling their home phones was useless if they weren't there, which was usually the case.

If I couldn't get in touch with the students to remind them about Wednesdays, I needed the help of someone in the household. When the parents came to me to complain about the attendance numbers, I assumed they'd be allies in improving the situation, so I asked them to remind their kids about coming. The response I got was "I can't make my kid come to church." Never mind that I never said a word about "making" them do anything. Is a reminder really such an unreasonable request?

Mostly what I really wanted was a feeling that the parents were working with me, that I wasn't in this alone. Instead, I felt I was being told that they planned to be gone every time I held an event, and they might come to a midweek gathering if they weren't busy and happened to think about it; yet I was solely to blame for the lack of attendance.

I began hearing rumors that some members of the youth group had been caught drinking. I soon became convinced that the parents wanted me to miraculously fix their kids - turn them instantly into straight-laced types who would say no to sex, drugs, and booze. Never mind that I hadn't had much time to get to know any of them and had, at best, a few hours a couple of days a week to make any sort of impact on them. I was the one on the hook for their behavior with parents unwilling to do anything other than argue with me about my scheduling and my need for a little help.

I began focusing more on the junior high students with

some success. Where the high school attendance was diminishing, junior high was nearly doubled - especially at the weekend events I put together. Wednesday nights with them were never lacking in participation. Somehow, my success there never seemed to matter to those complaining about the high school attendance.

Unfortunately, my biggest critics, the ones who wanted miracles that didn't require them to actually do anything, were also decision makers for the church board so my continued employment was largely up to them.

The pastor and I got along extremely well. His wife was a source of advice that has stuck with me ever since, such as viewing the responsibilities of a "pastor" as different from those of a "preacher." He, too, was feeling discouraged about how much the members of the congregation were resisting his attempts to lead them. He never mentioned names, but the writing on the wall suggested that his biggest roadblocks were many of the same decision makers who weren't happy with me.

The pastor got me involved with programs designed to help the church as a whole grow spiritually, but despite the training seminars we attended and initiatives we attempted to implement, when the time came to spend money on materials or to get people to give up some time outside of the standard Sunday morning services he was shut down. I can't say what happened at that place after I left, but during my time there I never saw any of his efforts amount to anything, no matter how hard he tried.

I don't mean to cast everyone at the church in the same light because I knew some of them prior and still know some of them now. We absolutely had some people there with their hearts in the right place, but too many of them seemed more concerned about appearances than anything else.

I call it "churchianity." It's a mindset of church as a social club. It's being worried about someone wearing the right clothes on Sunday morning instead of them hurting or searching for hope (a situation you can see demonstrated in the book and movie *Jesus Revolution* but that I've witnessed myself at several different churches). It's a do-as-I-say-not-as-I-do mentality that has parents wanting their kids to lead moral lives while they themselves demonstrate the opposite.

Rumors of drunken behavior, drug peddling (including selling to children), and other improprieties began to filter through the proverbial grapevine. How much of it is true I can't say, but in every case, they seemed to involve the very same parents who opposed the pastor and myself. If your lifestyle includes selling illegal drugs to kids while you call yourself a Christian on Sundays, it is not the fault of your church's youth pastor that your children are making poor life choices.

One of the most valuable experiences I took away from this church was that of preaching sermons behind the pulpit when the pastor was away. Public speaking comes easier to me than one-on-one interactions, and that's paved the way for opportunities for me to speak on discussion panels and at events. I've delivered sermons, spoken to rooms full of people about topics ranging from autism to the realism of religion in video games to how the writings of J.R.R. Tolkien compare to those of C.S. Lewis. My time with the Fans For Christ ministry has helped bring me out of my shell when it comes to interacting with people directly. Before any of that happened, my time with this church showed me that public speaking skills and a desire to help others don't automatically make one well-suited for a position like a minister of youth, which played a significant role in solidifying that shell around me.

My wife says that I would make a good counselor. If she's right, I think it has to do with three things: I have direct experiences with depression and autism that the average person doesn't, I've successfully endured abuse and betrayal that others are still trying to work through, and my vast collection of failures and bad decisions (many of which you're reading about in these pages) have shown me that I'm no better than anyone I might attempt to counsel. In other words, what I've encountered gives me a window into the plights of others and the humility to recognize that that could be, or may have been, me.

At the same time, I have a tendency to disconnect from people. I can empathize in a moment of emotion and then completely forget you were struggling. And that's assuming I was able to empathize at all. If you, too, are on the spectrum, there's a good chance you can relate to what I'm saying.

Cognitive dissonance in a nutshell might be described as this: I have knowledge that I know you don't have, but, when interacting with you, I don't always realize that you don't have it. If that doesn't make sense, you probably haven't experienced it. I didn't understand it myself until I took part in an exercise that demonstrated, much to my surprise, that I have it.

In this exercise I knew what to expect. In fact, I thought it was silly to think that I would treat someone as though they had knowledge that I knew they didn't have. And yet that's exactly what I did. I repeated the exercise and did it a second time.

I took part in that exercise a few years ago, so I've known this about myself for a while now and try to be mindful of it. Because of that, I was shocked to find out that I still do this without realizing it. I was describing the concept of cognitive dissonance to someone not long ago when my wife said, "Yeah, you do that to me all the time." I wasn't expecting that. Even knowing I do it and trying not to doesn't keep me from it. Thank God I have a patient wife.

These are all common traits of autism. I don't think they're great qualities for a youth minister to have. That's not to say that no person on the spectrum should ever do that job, it just wasn't a good fit for someone like me.

In my years since leaving that position, I have been a key member of the tech teams at other churches, and I've given a number of other pulpit sermons. Even so, I've never been on staff at another church, and I've never been involved with another youth group outside of providing some technical assistance. I think that shows that there is a place for me, a way to use my skills and talents, but much like when I took advanced History instead of English, it's been a matter of learning to use my strengths rather than dwell on my weaknesses. That's a lesson I wouldn't learn for a while yet. Sometimes I still wonder if I've learned it at all!

I wanted to believe I could accomplish anything I set my mind to, but I didn't need a dry fleece to prove I wasn't good at this job. I thought for a while that I would try to stick it out, if for no other reason than because I didn't know what else to do. It was when I got reprimanded for the low high school attendance that I knew, one way or another, my days there were numbered.

Don't complain to me about your glass being empty and then expect me to fill it while telling me that you didn't bother to bring it. If my drinks aren't the best, I'll own up to it, but I will not bear your part of the blame as if it were my own. The parents telling me their kids had better things to do than to come to church while simultaneously chiding me for those kids not being there was when I started thinking about my other options.

If my hopes for what I might've been able to accomplish at the church fell flat, my next job made that look insignificant by comparison.

8

Terrifying Textiles

I miss broadcasting. I fill that by helping with video production at my church on Sundays. I've helped out where I can in recent years with a few low-budget movies as both actor and producer, which has been rewarding in many ways (although a career in cinema has not been one of them). I didn't expect full-time ministry to pay more than television did, but I'd hoped it would be more fulfilling. With both of those options lying shattered on life's road, my parents talked me into pursuing a career in computers.

That ultimately proved to be a good choice for me, but at this time I had no idea how to break into a computer related field. I set my sights on working for a large textile company for two primary reasons. First of all, the company was based in my hometown. They were the largest employer in the area, so I figured there was a good chance they'd be hiring sooner or later.

Second of all, I had connections there. You could hardly live in my hometown without knowing someone who worked for this company, but I knew people with some influence. At least one of them thought I would be a good fit. He suggested I start by taking a job in one of the plants. That would show that I was serious about starting a career there, give me some first-hand knowledge of the industry, and provide an income for me while I worked out the long-term plan. I applied and was immediately hired.

On my first day I found out that my direct supervisor, the one who had interviewed and hired me, was to be out on sick leave for a short while. That "short while" turned out to be almost my entire time at the plant. I saw her maybe two or three times, which was a shame because she was the only fully competent person in charge there. While she was out, I was to report to another supervisor who, it turns out, had no business supervising anyone.

In this particular plant we made yarn that would be used to make cloth at various other plants. We had a machine that ate raw cotton like a ravenous creature. I always imagined that it was digesting the fluff to excrete the usable materials which would be spun into the yarn. This first part of the process was done underneath the main building in a series of dingy rooms that felt like Buffalo Bill's basement in the movie *The Silence of the Lambs*. Some of the walls were literally made of dirt. Thank

God there was no tub with a corpse in it, although I would hardly have been surprised to find such a thing.

The machine had a mouth full of huge teeth that sat in the first room. Its yards of intestines for moving the materials along the digestive tract sprawled throughout the winding basement. The dim light and dirty walls made it feel old and haunted, while the noise of the machine sounded like the deafening, unending roar of a hungry beast. One person had the job of feeding the masticating jaws and clearing any blockages that formed. Couldn't have the Beast getting constipated, now, could we?

It was a creepy and isolated job that I worked whenever the regular operator was out. It was the only job in that plant that I ever actually enjoyed doing.

The heart and soul of the plant was what we called "The Floor." Here, the Beast's excrement was put into machines that spun the raw materials into yarn which they then spooled on plastic tubes. Rows of machines dedicated to this job, each several yards long, filled a huge room.

I never knew much about those machines. The people who ran them were a dedicated and experienced team. I only ever dealt with the very beginning of the process, feeding the Beast, and the very end of it, getting the yarn ready to ship out. It was the end of the process that drove many workers into fits of rage.

At specific intervals, the spooled yarn had to be removed

from the back end of each machine. Those would be loaded onto special racks which were essentially heavy-duty, metal carts designed to hold multiple spools of thread. We called this "doffing." The Doffers would transfer the spools from the machines to the racks and then take the racks down a freight elevator to a large loading dock where they would be weighed, tagged, and stored until a truck came by to pick them up to take them on to the next plant.

That doesn't sound like a big deal, does it? It was a simple enough job, but it was physically demanding in ways that nobody prepared me, or anyone else, for.

You see, each machine would create multiple spools, and we had several machines. That meant a whole lot of spools to transfer. The size varied some, but they tended to be wide enough that if I put my thumb in the hole of the plastic spool and my fingers around the outer edge of the thread I could barely spread my hands wide enough to grip them. I never weighed any of them individually, but if I had to guess from memory, I would say that they probably averaged five or six pounds each. A five-pound spool of thread doesn't sound like a big deal until you have to transfer several dozen within a small window of time and then do the whole process over again a short while later, repeated until the end of a twelve-hour shift.

Imagine picking up a five-pound weight in each hand, turning around, and placing them on a shelf. Now do that twenty times as fast as you can, then do that ten times over the course of a day and you'll begin to get a taste of the demands of the doffing job.

I was reasonably fit in those days thanks to my history with Martial Arts and moderately active, but I was maybe 130 pounds soaking wet. I was small and definitely not muscular. My first few times working as a doffer left me unable to use my arms by quitting time. By the start of my next shift my muscles were already sore, meaning that I was starting at a disadvantage which only left me feeling worse for the shift after that. I spent my first several days off trying to use my arms as little as possible.

I was given the job of doffer because the guy before me got fed up and walked out. He'd been given the job because the guy before him had done the same thing. The problem wasn't just the physical demands of the job, lots of jobs are just as demanding or more so; it was the horrible working conditions that made a hard job unbearable.

The racks onto which we loaded spools were the big industrial types with two wheels in the middle and a wheel on each end so that as the weight caused the rack to rock back and forth, it would have support. These things were heavy when they were empty, so add a few hundred pounds of thread to them and they became a challenge even for the guys who were considerably larger than I was.

Now compound that challenge with the fact that many of them didn't roll like they should. It wasn't uncommon to get a rack with wheels so misshapen that two men working together couldn't budge it. When that happened, we had to find a pallet jack that could lift the weight and roll the rack using the assistance of a motor. "Why not use the pallet jack all the time?" you ask? Because we weren't the only ones who needed to use it. Access to it was never guaranteed. Every time we needed it, we had to spend several minutes searching for it only to discover, in many instances, that it wasn't available to us.

Moving those racks at all was hard enough, but we weren't just taking them from the main floor to the loading dock. First, we had to take each one to a scale to create a tracking sticker for it. After that they would finally get parked somewhere to await pickup, but even that part of the process was more difficult than it sounds.

Part of the trouble we ran into came by way of the truck schedule. It was sporadic at best. Lack of space in the shipping dock didn't mean we stopped spooling yarn, it only meant that the doffers had to make enough space to store the racks until a truck finally came by. Struggling to find enough room in the loading dock to fit all of our loaded racks was a common problem. The dock was huge, so we always found room somewhere, but that meant we were often dragging them the distance of a good-sized warehouse crowded with other racks.

Have you ever gotten a shopping cart that doesn't roll like it should? Now imagine that weighing a few hundred pounds, and you have to push it from one end of the store to the other. Now imagine you have three or four at a time which you have to move one after the other, and you have to do that multiple times throughout a whole day. And you have to do all that after transferring all those five-pound weights.

To hear management talk about the job of a doffer, it doesn't sound too unbearable if one could survive the physical demands: load the spools onto the racks, bring the racks down to the loading dock, and take a break until the next round of doffing – never mind how that downplays the difficulties or the time it took to deal with problems like racks that wouldn't roll. What they didn't tell us was how the job frequently kept us from having any down time at all.

When our loading dock was full of loaded racks that meant we had fewer empty ones for the next round of doffing. The machines didn't stop spooling for any reason, so a lack of empty racks did not mean a break for us. In fact, that actually meant more work.

Those same trucks that picked up our loaded racks also brought us the empty ones. If those trucks weren't bringing us empty racks, it fell to the doffers to travel to other plants in search of more. Keep in mind that the trucks not making their runs was already creating more work for us as we struggled to make room to store everything, now we had still more work that was beyond our job description.

Instead of having a moment to sit down after the loaded racks were put away, we immediately loaded ourselves into a truck and set off on our search. We had to be back before the next round of doffing began, so time was short. As an additional challenge, none of the other plants were guaranteed to have any empties at all meaning that we might have to travel between a few of them to find what we needed. Between my regular job responsibilities and the task of restocking racks, it wasn't uncommon for me to work a twelve hour shift with no break, not even for lunch.

To make matters worse, neither of us who worked as doffers had a permit to drive a big truck. We had one employee, a buddy of the supervisor's, who we had to call on to drive us around. That was it. He didn't have to do so much as get out of the driver's seat, much less help load any racks; he just had to drive the truck while we did the heavy lifting. If he didn't do this, we couldn't do our jobs which meant the people working the spooling machines couldn't do theirs, and yet he always acted like driving us was an imposition for which we were responsible.

I don't know what the actual job responsibilities of this man were because I don't remember ever seeing him do anything but sit in a chair talking to his buddy, the supervisor. But to drive us around so that we could fill what little free time we had with additional work was asking a favor that he would begrudgingly do, despite us having no other options. He treated us like he was doing us a personal favor that he didn't really want to do, for which we should be humbly grateful.

The truck driver's attitude, our aggravation over the working conditions, and the supervisor's preferential treatment of his friend finally came to an explosive confrontation. On this night, my doffing partner and I were low on empty racks as per usual. We'd been doing the job long enough to have learned something about the schedules of the trucks coming in and which ones were more likely to bring us empty racks. We reasoned that if we took our truck to retrieve racks from one specific plant, the scheduled pickup from a different one was likely to bring us an additional load of empties.

The catch was that the plant due to pick up was close by while the other one, the one to which we wanted to take our truck, was further away. We reasoned that if the truck coming in brought us empties after we'd retrieved a load ourselves, that gave us two loads to work with while only making one trip out. If the truck didn't bring us any empties, then we had to make a second trip either way.

Our gamble proved to be a wise one. The truck from the closer plant brought us a load of racks, we saved making a second trip, and everyone, including our truck driver, had to do less work. Our driver, however, was furious that we'd made him drive to the furthest plant without going to the closer one first. He complained to the supervisor, who confronted us in a rage.

The supervisor demanded to know why we'd gone to the distant plant instead of the closer one. We explained our reasoning and told him that it had paid off. I expected him to say,

"Oh, well I guess that was a good idea after all." I thought he might even say, "Good job saving everyone from having to do unnecessary work." Instead, he responded that he didn't care. We were to do what the truck driver said to do because if we didn't, he wouldn't drive us anymore.

I typically avoid confrontation as much as possible. As much as I hate to admit it, that means you can push me around to some extent. I'll suffer through it to keep the peace... until I hit my breaking point. This was my breaking point. I told my supervisor that the plant couldn't run without those racks and neither of us could legally drive a truck, so if his buddy didn't want to drive us then we'd be more than happy to get to sit down for a few minutes and let him explain to his boss why the plant wasn't running.

I have never in my life told off a boss like I did this man. We'd done something good, and he was treating us like we'd caused a disaster. I was tired, angry, and insulted. Better yet, I was right and he couldn't argue the point. He stormed off without another word and never confronted me again, but I also didn't work there for much longer after that. I was at the end of my tolerance with this place; if there was any doubt that I couldn't work for this man that reprimand had removed it.

This wasn't the first clash I'd had with him; I'd just not pushed very hard before. I'd already confronted him and one or two of the other supervisors about the fact that I was routinely working twelve-hour shifts with no breaks for lunch. That was, of course, against the law, and their response of "suck it up and eat in the truck" (meaning they expected me to eat my lunch while being driven to pick up a load of empty racks, which does **not** qualify as a thirty minute lunch break, never mind the mandated fifteen minute breaks which were a rare treat even on a good night) convinced me that they didn't care at all about how hard they were pushing us. The only reason I didn't press the matter was because I still aspired to work for the company in their office environment. Getting them into legal trouble didn't seem conducive to that goal.

The next nail in the proverbial coffin of my time at the plant came shortly after the lunch break confrontation. I can't remember if this was before or after the incident with the rack pickup, because they all happened so closely together and so close to the end of my time there that the exact sequence of events is a bit of a blur.

I was so stressed and so physically exhausted that I got sick. During my shift, I would doff a few spools of yarn then run outside to throw up in the bushes (I couldn't make it as far as the toilets). Back inside, I'd go to doff more yarn then back outside to vomit again. Because I had no breaks to eat, I had nothing solid to vomit - what came out of me was nothing but Gatorade which was the only thing I had time to consume between doffing and rack hunting. I told that same supervisor I was sick, and he told me to get back to work. Maybe I should have just vomited where I stood so that he would take me seriously.

Here, once again, I tried to suck up the mistreatment to protect what I hoped would be my future at the company. However, my decision to leave became an easy one after the final insult.

Nobody had informed me that the plant routinely closed down for the winter. As we prepared to close for what I assumed was a temporary Christmas break, I was already making plans to use that time to find other employment. To my disbelief, I was informed that the shutdown was for the duration of the winter months, not just a Christmas break. This was water cooler talk between coworkers, not information given to me by management.

I asked what we were supposed to do in the meantime and was told to file for unemployment. I had no intention of doing any such thing because I had no intention of stepping foot in that plant ever again. When my shift ended, I walked out the door without bothering to speak a word to my supervisor even to tell him that I wouldn't be returning.

I still made an attempt to join the company's staff of office workers in Atlanta, Georgia, but when I was late to my interview because I was on Peachtree Rd. instead of Peachtree Rd. North, (or something like that) I failed to make a good impression. My motivation to work for them at all was hanging on by a thread (if you'll pardon the pun) so I didn't put much effort into swaying them towards hiring me.

Even though I didn't join the company's Atlanta office,

I still ended up moving to Georgia for my next job, so I quickly lost touch with everyone connected to the plant. I'd made some friends there, but the three bad employment experiences I'd had since moving back to my hometown after college (including the TV station and the church) caused me to cut ties with basically everyone who wasn't a relative, a member of my childhood church (not the one that hired me as a youth minister), or a friend from high school.

I did hear a rumor that when the plant resumed operation that next spring, the supervisor that had given me so much trouble, as well as one or two others who were in league with him in other departments, were demoted. I guess driving at least three people to quit without notice (and possibly more considering that my doffing partner was also talking about leaving) in under six months finally got someone's attention.

Despite my horrendous treatment at this place, it was a unique experience in my life. It taught me the value of standing up for myself in the face of mistreatment. If I were to have that confrontation about the lack of a lunch break now, I would be a lot more inclined to respond to "eat in the truck and deal with it" with something much closer to "let's see what my lawyer has to say about that."

I have only one true regret about my time there - missing out on the opportunity to be in a Mel Gibson movie. I was pursuing some acting work during that time and even had an agent. The highlight of that experience was getting to work with

Meat Loaf Aday, about whom I could never say enough nice things. He was a wonderful man, and I was a fool to not ask if I could get a picture with him.

During my time at the plant my agent got me a job on a movie called "The Patriot." I don't know what the part might have been, but I was told it was to be a speaking role. I don't think I knew it was a Mel Gibson movie at that time, because if I had I might've made a different decision. I asked for time off work and was denied. I begged and was told no again like I was a child wanting candy at a grocery store. If I'd known how things with the company were going to turn out, I would've gone anyway and let the company fire me if they were so inclined. Once again, I didn't want to do anything to jeopardize my potential employment with the company's office staff, so I made the safe choice.

That wouldn't be the last time I walked away from a job without warning anyone (you'll soon read about the other), but it is the only one I look back on wondering if I should've considered legal action. If this is the kind of treatment other employees endured, it's no wonder that the company faced hard times not long after.

I've had people in my life who have treated me as if any credibility I have when it comes to other people is worthless because of my autism. Others tell me the opposite, but sometimes the words of the critics ring louder than anyone else, and so I wonder if someone who's better with social interactions could have turned a job situation like the textile plant into something less traumatic by handling the people involved differently than I did.

That's my first thought. Then I look back on the experience: the complete disregard for the workers, the willingness to ignore labor laws, preferential treatment so severe that it led someone to get angry over a situation that benefited everyone involved but lightly stepped on someone's toes in the process. That's a bad situation no matter who you are or how you handle it. Not every problem I run into with other people is because I'm an autistic introvert. Sometimes it has nothing at all to do with me. Sometimes people are just jerks. They're probably jerks to most of the people around them. Sometimes it's better to get out of a situation rather than try to fix it.

Thank God I got out of that situation. Unfortunately, things got worse before they got better.

9

Cult of Salesmanship

I first moved to Atlanta, Georgia with the intention of joining the ranks of the same company that owned the textile plant. That was the whole purpose of enduring that job, to act as a stepping stone to something better. I wasn't especially happy with the company after my treatment at the plant, but I was sticking to the plan if only because I didn't have any better options. Since I had no intention of stepping foot inside that building ever again, it was now or never for the next stage: apply for a job at the head office. So off to Georgia I went.

Up until Atlanta, the largest city in which I'd lived was Mobile, Alabama. I was strictly small-town, so I wasn't prepared for the multiple interstates and bumper-to-bumper rush hour traffic. I've now lived here for more of my life than I've been anywhere else, and I'm still not used to it. I don't drive through downtown Atlanta if I can help it.

My second time in the city, I mixed up I-85 and I-285. For those of you not familiar with Atlanta's layout, we have two interstates that run North and South. These are 75 and 85. We also have a big, round racetrack known as The Perimeter. This is 285. It connects with both 75 and 85 south of Atlanta and then again on the north side. I knew enough to know I was supposed to be on one of the 85s, but I didn't know that there were two roads that included the number 85 until I had to make a split-second decision about which one I was supposed to be taking.

We didn't have mobile GPS apps on our phones during those ancient times. We used services like MapQuest to print out directions, which we followed like pirates using a treasure map. When I realized I was facing a decision to choose between 85 and 285, I didn't have enough time to check my printed directions before I had to take one or the other. I was supposed to be going South, which 285 does (until it curves back around to go North again), so I thought I was fine until it connected with I-85 the second time. Didn't I just pass the 85/285 junction? How could I be at it again? I was beyond confused. Fortunately, I'd gotten on 285 at the North side, so when it reconnected with 85 on the South end, I was able to get back on track without going too far out of my way. I paid closer attention to the interstate layout after that.

The other thing you need to know about Atlanta roads

before moving here is that half of them are named Peachtree. We've got Peachtree Rd. which parallels New Peachtree Rd. for a while. To stay on Peachtree Rd, you have to take a right at some point. If you keep going straight, you'll find yourself on Peachtree Blvd. which becomes Peachtree Industrial Blvd, which then splits to create Peachtree Pkwy. with a different Peachtree Blvd. (which is also Peachtree Place Pkwy. - a completely different Peachtree Parkway than the one I've already mentioned) branching off not long after Peachtree Square. If you think I'm exaggerating, please read that paragraph again with a map open.

I avoid that whole area not only because it's convoluted to the point of feeling like a Monty Python sketch, but also because I get so tired of hearing the word "peachtree" (especially when you add into the mix all the businesses that incorporate the word) that I want to plug my ears and yell, "La la la la la!" just to push the sound out of my mind.

With no GPS and no idea what I was getting into with Atlanta's convoluted layout, I managed to get myself quite lost looking for the building where I was to be interviewed. All these years later I don't remember exactly which roads go with my story, but if I was looking for the address on Peachtree Rd, I was supposed to be on Peachtree Blvd. (or something like that).

These roads are full of buildings, so when I didn't see the correct address my first assumption was that I had overlooked it, not that I was on the wrong road. I turned around to retrace my path. Then I did it again. Where was this place?

Yes, kids, we did have cell phones in those long-ago days, but not every single person had one yet. I was one of the have-nots because I was a have-not in the job department. I had to find a place with a public phone where I could stop and call my prospective employer. They immediately saw my mistake and gave me directions on how to get from where I was to where I needed to be.

I arrived at the interview extremely late. I don't know if that's the reason I wasn't offered a job, but it certainly didn't help my chances. Maybe they didn't have faith in someone who couldn't locate a simple address. Maybe they felt like I should've left earlier to give myself more time to arrive when I was supposed to, never mind that getting lost in a maze of roads all named the same thing isn't something a person new to the big city can be reasonably expected to anticipate. I tried to downplay my nightmare at the textile plant, but I doubt they would've looked favorably on finding out that I'd left without bothering to tell my previous supervisor so much as "stick it where the sun don't shine!" For all I know, maybe they talked to that supervisor and he told them that I didn't follow instructions well while conveniently leaving out the part about him denying me a lunch break during my twelve hour shifts, or him trying to force me to take on unnecessary extra work so that his buddy could warm the seat of a chair instead of putting forth a small amount of effort for half an hour.

Whatever the reason may be, I didn't get the office job that had been my goal from the day I decided to apply for the textile position. All of that aggravation - working myself sick, missing out on being in a movie with Mel Gibson, refraining from making a stink about them breaking labor laws - amounted to absolutely nothing.

I didn't lose a bit of sleep over not working for that company, but I now found myself once again in the position of having no career path. I had no confidence in finding a good job in broadcasting. Although that didn't stop me from looking, it wasn't with the same passion I'd once had. I was still willing to consider work in the computer field, but I was back to square one on where to start.

All I knew for sure was that my small hometown held few opportunities for me. My three attempts at starting a career there (in three vastly different fields) had been utter disasters. One way or another, I wanted to find a job in or near Atlanta both because of the prospect of more options and because my girlfriend would be attending college in North Georgia. I wanted to be closer to her than Alabama was.

The reason I'm saying so much about my situation is because without that context, my next job choice would be criticized as poor, out-of-character writing if I were fictional. I was willing to take just about any job I could find if it meant I could get myself established in Georgia. If I could afford a place to live and food for my belly, I could figure the rest out later. So in one of the more absurd decisions I've ever made, I took a job as a door-to-door salesman.

To be fair to myself, I didn't realize at first that I was taking a door-to-door sales job. The company promoted itself as an advertising business. "Advertising" was even part of the name. I was expecting to do creative things there: write marketing lines ("Try our zombie fingers! Just don't ask what the sweet'n'sour sauce is made of." (That's a joke from one of my horror novels.)), maybe do some visual layouts, or, if I was really lucky, edit and maybe even produce some radio and TV spots. I didn't know what they did at this "advertising" company. I was willing to try just about anything, but if I'd known it was a sales position I probably wouldn't have bothered with it. By the time I realized what I was getting into, I'd been offered the job and needed the money enough to not turn it down.

I must preemptively ask your forgiveness before this next part of the story. I'm about to be vague. I need to tell you something about the name of this place without actually saying the name because I'm going to be slinging some ugly mud at them. I don't think they're still around to care, but I don't want to take that chance.

The owner came up with the company name by combining the initials of his kids' names (a fact which I learned prior to taking the job). The result was the same name as a false god from the Old Testament. As an extreme example, imagine someone innocently combining letters and, without realizing the significance of what they were doing, naming their company SATAN.

The name alone almost stopped me from going to the interview. Maybe it should've, except then I wouldn't have such interesting stories to write now.

The structure of the company was not unlike a sort of pyramid scheme. Person A, the owner of the company, brought in Person B who then recruited me along with a few others. Person B would get a share of my profits while Person A got a share of his. Eventually I would, theoretically, have people under me so my profitability would likewise increase. The more people I recruited, the more potential I would have for residual income from their sales, and a portion of that money would trickle up. I have to assume that the amount would diminish as it passed through more people, but ideally the owner would eventually have a massive salesforce, so even if his cut was smaller coming from the lower tier people it would be from enough sources to add up.

I'm making some assumptions here because none of it worked out as promised, and I'm not aware of any person from my tier actually ever recruiting anyone under them. Most of the people hired at the same time I was left before I did. I know that others didn't stick around either because I had a chance meeting with a person from the company years later, but I'll save that encounter for the end of the story. For now, I'll just say that she was one of their most accomplished and successful salespeople.

If she couldn't make the scheme work for her, I doubt anyone could have. Seeing as how I can't currently find any proof that the company ever existed, I'd be willing to bet it didn't survive for very long as more people discovered their empty promises and fled.

Those top tier people, the guy who recruited me and the owner of the company, were excellent salesmen so it probably goes without saying that they were charismatic, personable, energetic, fun guys. They knew how to say the right things, guide you where they wanted you to go, and manipulate their sales force into chasing pipedreams. To this day, I'm not entirely certain how much of what they said was actually a lie and how much was them leading me to think I'd heard something I never did - kind of like how people will comment on how violent the end of the movie *Braveheart* is when the entire execution scene shows little more than Mel Gibson's reactions to what's happening to him, or how *Reservoir Dogs* leaves viewers convinced they've seen a graphically gory scene of an ear being cut off when the camera actually pans away from the violence.

After an excellent interview with the owner, I walked away feeling positive about the job. I was dazzled by dreams of riches. I had no aspirations to be a salesman, of course, but since I had experience with retail, I thought I could suffer through it long enough to recruit a sales team under me after which I'd be able to relax with the salesman part of the job and enjoy the trickle-up income. It was either that or work there only long enough to find a better job. Either option seemed like a win.

And here is one of those moments when I'm not entirely sure if I was fed an actual lie, or if I got the wrong idea through a carefully worded sleight of hand. I thought I was going to be making a guaranteed flat income plus commissions, much like my electronics retail job. I didn't find out until after I'd taken the job that I was working on commissions only. If I didn't make any sales, I didn't get paid! Being the non-salesman that I am, that was concerning, but the top-tier guys assured me, assured us all, that the money was going to pour in. They convinced me to stick with it.

To the surprise of absolutely no one that knows me, my sales were never great. Even so, I did make some money. It wasn't much, but I'd only just started so I just needed to give it more time. Right?

By the second paycheck I was doing better with my sales, so I expected a decent return in my pay. What I got was a pittance. Part of the sales pitch for taking the job was that I'd be able to write off gas, meals, and other such essentials when it came time for taxes. But that wasn't going to do me any good if I couldn't afford gas and food until then. What good are dreams of riches if you can't survive in the meantime?

One thing I liked about the job was the people. I connected with one girl because she'd once dated a friend of mine from high school. What are the odds of that? We were hours from my hometown, in an entirely different state, and yet we had a mutual friend. Another girl and I bonded over our shared love of the same obscure band, Fleming & John. The guy who recruited me took me out for beers from time to time, and even though I didn't drink at all at that time, he always offered to cover whatever I did get (probably Coca-Cola since that was my drink of choice back when I still drank soda).

Everyone was friendly, encouraging, and upbeat. Far from being competitive, trying to snatch sales for ourselves out of the hands of others, we all worked hard to help each other succeed. We even took sales trips carpooling and sharing hotel rooms so that we could take advantage of untapped markets. We were the people knocking on your door telling you about the reasons you should buy our vacuum cleaners (or whatever it was we sold - I must've blocked it from my memory because try as I might, I can't recall one single product I ever handled at this place).

I even tried to make a sale in a strip club, less because I expected to be able to and more because we were told to knock on every single door. It's the one and only time I've been in such a club, and my eyes nearly fell out of my head in the thirty seconds or so that it took for the bouncer to send me on my way (he was very decent to me, though very firm that I was not going to be selling anything there).

I wasn't the only person having trouble making ends meet in these early days of building up the sales force. The big boss had a solution by way of a house with a large basement. He was willing to let us crash there while we got our feet underneath us. I slept on a used (but as far as I could tell, clean) mattress on the floor, but I had a roof, a shower, and even an occasional meal thanks to the guy's wife cooking for us all periodically. I assumed that the boss was willing to do this for us because if he got us to the point of making good money, then he got paid, too. Now I think it was nothing more than another part of the scheme.

That dangling carrot of dreaming about what we'd do with all the money we'd have when we hit the big time was getting harder and harder to see through the haze of living in some guy's basement with four or five other people, hoping I could make enough in my next paycheck to buy enough gas to get to work and back every day.

I quickly made up my mind to start hunting for another job rather than stick this one out. Since we were out in the wild all day every day, I felt certain that I could find time to check newspapers and help wanted postings, sneak away to make calls, and maybe even make some contacts. I quickly came to realize just how tight the reins were on us. Being in groups like we were made it tough to do anything at all without being observed, not just by the rest of the team but also by the team leaders.

We started early in the morning and finished late in the afternoon. When the sales day was over, we still had the daily office wrap-up. This was essentially a company-wide meeting but was, in a lot of ways, a sort of pep rally. We gathered in a big circle to talk about the day and plan for the next one. If we hit certain sales milestones, we rang a bell and ran around the circle high-fiving everyone. At first, on the surface, it looked like a way to keep spirits high, encourage us during the hard times, and motivate us to do well. I began seeing it in a different light when I discovered how difficult it was to get any time to myself.

The meetings really were the best part of any given day - gathering with people who generally liked each other to hang out for a while and encourage each other. But they also added an hour or more onto an already full workday. After a particularly long, hot day with a lot of walking I returned to the office physically exhausted. I leaned against a wall to rest for a few minutes (there were no chairs for us there) and was immediately chastised. Being upbeat and energetic was not optional, it was demanded. Ringing the bell and running the achievement circle was not optional. Cheering each other on about how much money was going to be dripping off of us in the near future was not optional. The "Weird Al" Yankovic album title "Mandatory Fun" comes to mind when thinking about these meetings.

That rang a different kind of bell for me - it was the tolling for the end of my time as a salesman. I realized that these people had a complete monopoly of my time. I worked long hours with them every day which I would expect with any job, but then I had no choice but to give up a large chunk of what should've been my own free time after work to attend these pep rally meetings, after which I went to sleep in the boss's basement. Even when driving between the house and the office I always had someone riding with me. There was no time to get away, and I can't help but think that it was a deliberate part of the whole design. If we had no time to ourselves, then we couldn't hunt for other jobs.

I was teetering on the edge of going from disillusioned to feeling trapped when an interaction drove the final nail in the coffin. The #2 guy, the one who'd recruited me, and who I might've considered a friend if circumstances had been different, took me out for beers. I remember more about his side of the conversation than my own. In my memory, he reminds me of actor Peter Riegert (best known to me as Lt. Kellaway from *The Mask*) although that may just be my mind playing tricks on me. In my mind's eye I remember "Peter" and me sitting at a table in a pub, him with a couple of beer bottles, me with a Coke, discussing the future.

Remember me mentioning the carrot dangling before us to keep us hungry for it? That carrot was our dream of what we'd do with the promised future riches. In the office, we had a bulletin board where everyone pinned an image of their ultimate goal. We had lots of pictures of fancy cars, boats, huge houses with pools, and other lofty possessions. We were encouraged to dream big and to look frequently upon what we would one day own. I don't remember what mine was. It might've been a Lamborghini. If I had an absurd amount of money to spend on a car that I don't really need, that's what I'd own. I blame *Miami*

Vice for my Lamb fixation.

Of course, it didn't stop with a picture on a bulletin board; they had us talk about what we would own every chance they got. They wanted us fixated on that goal. Owning a Lamb, or a yacht, or a huge house would make us want to work for it but also keep us believing that we could achieve it through this company.

So, Peter (his real name also has a *Miami Vice* connection, but I won't mention it) and I were at the table when he started talking to me once again about what I would do with all my future money. This wasn't a picture tacked to a board; this was two people talking, so I got more personal with him. I don't remember exactly what I said to him, but I know I mentioned giving money to my church, helping family with whatever debts they had, and finding a nice place to live because I hoped to be providing a good home for my girlfriend at some point if we ever got married.

I may not remember exactly what I said, but I can quote his response verbatim: "You're a good man, Chad." It wasn't the words he said but how he said them that got me.

A common trait of people on the autism spectrum is that we tend to not read people well. I've often thought someone was joking when they weren't and didn't realize they were joking when they were. I've thought I was in trouble when I was being heralded, and I used to get on my ex-wife's nerves because I frequently thought she was upset with me when she was actually upset with other people while also thinking she was mad at other people when it was actually me she wanted to smack - one way or another I never seemed to get it right.

Looking back on the many times I've gotten someone's intentions wrong, I've learned to mistrust my perception of such things. I consider myself an unreliable narrator when it comes to body language, but not in this case. I have no doubts at all that I got this one right. I've spent quite a lot of time considering it.

"You're a good man, Chad," he said in a low voice. His head dropped like he couldn't look me in the eye. That was the end of the conversation. I can't help but think that at that moment his conscience was bothering him, that he couldn't stand the thought of what he was doing to me. As we drove back to the boss's basement, I made up my mind to leave.

I talked to my parents the next day and told them everything that was going on. My mother wasn't sure the group would let me go if they knew my plans. She was worried. It might've been different if I were living in my own place and could just not show up for work the next day, but I lived in the boss's house surrounded by people invested in the company.

I decided that I wouldn't just leave, I would vanish. I didn't have much there, but I had to have changes of clothes - nice ones at that, I was a salesman, after all. I'm not one to go long without a book at my side, and of course I had toiletries and such. I announced my plans for a weekend trip home to visit my parents, using the excuse of doing laundry to explain why I was taking all of my clothes (because that was just one of the questions they asked me). Were they curious about my plans because it's human nature to wonder, or were they trying to make sure they didn't lose their grip on me? I didn't want to find out. I didn't even care if I got my last paycheck since it would surely be just as miniscule as all the others.

If I hadn't already made my plans, the next insult would've pushed me over the edge. I didn't assume that I was living in the boss's basement for free, I was told directly that this was a rent-free situation. The only thing I assumed was the motivation behind the offer. A few days before my "disappearance," Peter came to all of us that called the basement our temporary home. He wanted us all to chip in a little money to help with expenses since we were using the boss's water and eating his food. I thought it was a nice gesture, and I didn't mind kicking in a few bucks as a show of gratitude. Except Peter wasn't asking for a couple of bucks, he was asking for a couple of hundred bucks from each of us. Not only was I not there long enough to use up a couple of hundred dollars' worth of water and food, but I also wasn't making enough money from this job to pay that even if I wanted to. I gave a noncommittal response to the request and silently thanked God that I'd already made my plans to vanish.

As I packed my car after work that last Friday, I said my goodbyes acting the part of someone who'd be back next Monday and left the world of door-to-door sales behind forever.

When tax time rolled around, I discovered that what they filed for my earnings said that I made considerably more money than I ever saw. Were they lying, or were they keeping that much of my money for themselves? I never found out. I got some help sorting that all out with a tax pro and wondered what had made me think that sales had ever been a good idea. The false god name should have been a dead giveaway.

Years later, I ran into one of the girls I worked with at the "advertising" company. She was a waitress at a restaurant I visited. I remembered her name because it was the same first and last name as a character from a popular TV show. I asked if she was who I thought she was when she came to take our order (I was there with my wife). She said she was but didn't remember me. I was surprised about that because she and I had shared car rides, hotel rooms (with other people, not the two of us alone), and numerous conversations. This was the same person who'd dated my high school friend, so we had that connection as well. Before I could remind her of who I was, she excused herself and never returned. A different waiter came to serve us.

I'd always wanted to talk to one of the other salespeople to see how much their experiences matched up with mine, and now here was not only a person who had been there after my departure, but also the only person with whom I had any connection outside of the company. When I saw her at the restaurant, which was close to where I lived at the time, meaning that she and I may very well have moved to the same little town in north Georgia, I initially thought that we might become friends again. How long had she stuck it out? Did she leave for the same reasons I did? I wanted to compare war stories. I had no idea that speaking to her would cause her to run off.

I've wondered about that encounter ever since. If she really didn't recognize me, did I somehow come off as creepy? I'm not sure how I would have. I was having dinner with my wife; I wasn't some shifty guy eyeballing her from the darkest corner of the room. We never got past me asking about her name so I never had the chance to ask her a question she could've found uncomfortable or offensive. Could me knowing her name be so creepy that she couldn't even give me the chance to remind her of our connection?

Did she lie? But if she knew who I was, then why would that make her not only unwilling to talk to me but also unwilling to do her job as a waitress? Was her time at that place so traumatic that she couldn't be in the same room with anyone connected to it? Even though I was nothing but a lowly salesman, there for a short while and then gone without a trace, was that enough of a connection? Did she bear me some kind of grudge for vanishing without saying something to her? That would be a lot of years to harbor feelings so strong as to make her never speak to me again.

One other possibility strikes me. It seems very conspiracy theoretical, but it makes as much sense to me as any other explanation for her behavior. What if she was afraid? What if, like me, she'd vanished, and now here was someone from those days randomly showing up at her new job asking about her name? What if she thought I was tracking her?

There's also the possibility that the bosses concocted some lie about me to explain my absence. I can't imagine what they could have told her to make her afraid of me for years to come, but none of my plausible explanations justify her reaction to my satisfaction.

That was, without a doubt, the strangest work experience of my life. Judging by the bizarre reaction the waitress had to me, I'm willing to bet I'm not the only one to say that. I've searched the internet for information on the company and come up with nothing. The only person whose full name I remember is the one I ran into at the restaurant, but her name is too common (if she even still has the same last name) for a social media search to be of much use for tracking her down (not that I would attempt to contact her after so perplexing an encounter). It's been over twenty years now, so even if I did run into someone from those days there's a good chance we wouldn't recognize each other. I guess I'll never know anything about what happened to the people there. I can only hope they all got out and went on to better things.

I close that chapter of my life with a life lesson: don't work for a false god.

10

Tech Hotel

After leaving my job as a salesman, if you can call that dip into the Twilight Zone a "job," I bounced around for a short while doing this and that. My most fun excursion from that time was working as a party DJ. The company that hired me provided all the equipment and set up the jobs. I would load the speakers, mixer, cables, and such in my car (it just barely fit in my sporty Saturn), transport it all to the venue, set it up, spin tunes and make announcements until the party ended, then bring everything back to the office and go home.

It really was a fun job. Having been a club and radio DJ, I was in my element even though I had to deal with people a lot. I hosted mostly wedding receptions with one odd side job for a small Republican political convention. I always looked for opportunities to play some of my more obscure music, which never got me a more enthusiastic response than when I played This Train's rendition of "I Saw the Light" (the Hank Williams song) at the political convention. For the rest of the day, I was explaining to people who This Train was and where they might be able to find the album, since Amazon hadn't yet revolutionized online purchasing.

Thinking back on those days, I'm almost disappointed that I don't have any interesting stories, which is why this job doesn't get its own chapter. I saw a lot of people looking like idiots doing the "Chicken Dance," the "Electric Slide," the "Locomotion," and any number of other ridiculous line dances that you'll still find at those kinds of parties. As much as I don't care to line dance, even I let my wife drag me out onto the dance floor to make a fool of myself every now and then. But as goofy as people got with their dancing, I never saw anyone accidentally rip the bride's dress off or drink from a broken wine bottle or any of the other horror stories I've heard from my friends. I never had any absurd demands, people not wanting to pay, or dancers getting so sloshed they couldn't stand up. I usually got tipped well and even had a number of people call the head office to voice their appreciation for my work. In short, I can't complain, which is a good thing for living a stress-free life but not for telling stories of crazy experiences.

One of my fondest memories from that time is playing the states against one another. If the group seemed to have a good sense of humor, I would talk about being an Alabama boy living in Georgia. Then I would play "Sweet Home Alabama" and "The Devil Went Down to Georgia" back-to-back.

If I hadn't moved so far away from the central office I might've kept going a while longer. It wasn't a career, but it was a decent bonus income and I had fun with it. Now that I think about it, that's probably what gave me the inspiration to look for what would become my first real job in Georgia. It provided something useful for my new resume, too, because I was about to put my skills to work for a major hotel chain.

If you've never been in or paid attention to some of the larger hotels (Hyatt, Marriott, Hilton, etc.) they often provide meeting rooms for rental. Depending on the size of the place, they might have enough space to make them feel like a small convention hall. The hotels that host Dragon*Con, for example, have multiple floors of meeting rooms, ballrooms, wide open areas for vendors and artists - all the space we need to hold a convention attended by tens of thousands of people spread out around a handful of hotels.

I don't know if this is still common, but years ago some of these places would hire an in-house audio/video team. I'll call us "AV" from here on out. I'm not going to tell you which chain I worked for because I would never want to work for them again, and I'm going to tell you exactly why at the end of this story, so I'll play it safe and try to not be too revealing.

As the in-house AV team, we handled everything you

might find for the business or technical side of a meeting or party. Tables and chairs were handled by others, anything dealing with food or beverages was its own department, anything else was most likely by or through us. From the high-tech items like projectors and complete sound systems (sometimes complex enough to require a dedicated sound engineer to run it all) to simple items like paper with markers; we set up, maintained, and were experts in all of it, which could be a challenge when getting someone's outdated laptop to send a signal to the projector they'd rented. We had two or three different storage rooms full of the various things we handled, and we occasionally had to rent more for the really big events.

High expectations were placed on us knowing everything about our technology, adhering to safety guidelines, and kissing our clients' butts. We were at the beck and call of the clients, providing technical support and any additional equipment they needed at a moment's notice. It was very much a customer-is-always-right situation with our job security dependent at least partially on customer satisfaction.

That may sound worse than it actually was. The more I look back on these experiences the more I see this pattern: it was usually our own sales people and coworkers, not the clients, who made the most ridiculous demands then fought us when we tried to explain to them that you can't put a twelve foot high screen in a room with a ten foot ceiling (I'm pulling those measurements out of the air, I don't remember the actual dimensions of the rooms).

It was, for the most part, a decent job. It could be hard work when it came to some of the huge events we hosted, the hours could keep me there until well after midnight (we had early and late shifts to keep anyone from having to work crazy long hours even though we all still had to do that from time to time), and it didn't pay especially well. At the same time, it was steady work with equipment and skill sets that I found comfortable, and I got along with the guys so well that some of us remain friends to this day.

One significant highlight of the job was the day that management decided to capitalize on my experience as a video editor. They bought an editing suite and offered my services to everyone from our own in-house projects to presentation videos for companies like Coca-Cola (who liked my work enough to be repeat customers). I don't know how much money we made off of that because I never saw any of it, but I had fun doing it.

I occasionally got into trouble for using footage of people who didn't want to be on screen. That taught me the value of my power; I'm controlling how viewers see you if I'm directing or editing a production. I decided that I don't care if I love you or hate your guts, if you're in front of a camera I control I'm going to make you look as good as I possibly can.

We occasionally bumped elbows with celebrities. I narrowly missed getting to meet the comedian Sinbad, but I did get to experience a private concert AC/DC performed for their record executives. I wouldn't be surprised if this was the smallest show they've ever done since achieving rock legend status. It was certainly miniscule compared to the packed-out arenas I know they've played. There were no props, fireworks, or cannons, just them on a stage with their instruments and a microphone, and they were mind-blowingly phenomenal.

A few different popular bands (most of whom I don't remember) were performing at the event over the course of a few days. They were the equivalent of the opening act for AC/DC. We were told by management that we weren't allowed in the ballroom where the bands were performing. For Collective Soul, a few of us hid in a service hallway so we could listen. For AC/DC, most of us on the AV staff were willing to risk getting in trouble if it meant getting to actually see them. We quietly slipped into the back of the room to watch Angus Young tune his guitar, hiding in the shadows, hoping no one threw us out.

It turns out we didn't have to worry about anything. In what I suspect was typical behavior for them, AC/DC didn't care what management said, they wanted an audience. They sent a guy into the hallway to invite anyone and everyone to come and enjoy the show. And they made sure we got a show we would be talking about for the rest of our lives. I have concerts of theirs on DVD, and they put no less energy into playing for a small crowd than they have for a crowd of thousands. From classics like "Back in Black" to songs from their newest album, they wanted us to sing along with them. "Don't be shy!" they said. It was a short 5-song set, but the eight-and-a-half-minute finale of "Let There Be Rock" was rock & roll heaven.

Unfortunately, all of the bands used outside AV rather than us. I figure they probably had seasoned concert techs who have forgotten more than I ever knew, therefore they didn't need a mere hotel staff tech. Just the same, we would all have jumped at the chance to work alongside them even if it had been in a more observational capacity.

We did have the opportunity to work with another musician. She wasn't as well-known as AC/DC or Collective Soul. As a matter of fact, I can't even remember her name. She had toured with someone notable (I want to say it was Stevie Wonder, but I could be wrong) and was better known for her connection with him than for her own music. Even so, you don't play for someone like Stevie if you can't play music.

She had her own AV techs, but she was relying primarily on our in-house services for her equipment needs. Her setup wasn't the most elaborate we ever did, but it was enough to fill up our atrium where she'd be performing for the pleasure of anyone passing through.

We had her ready for her sound check with time to spare. She was a celebrity, minor or not, so we wanted to make a good impression not only on her but on all of the hotel higher-ups that we expected would come listen to her. It wasn't often that we had the opportunity to put our skills on display for people who weren't directly involved with whatever event was taking place, because most of the time those events were behind closed doors. Out here in the open, for all eyes to see, we wanted to shine as brightly as we possibly could.

We weren't expecting any major problems during the sound check, but there's a reason a tech worth his/her pay tests the equipment before the show. Ever had your air conditioner work fine one day and die the next? Or maybe your car that ran fine yesterday won't start today. Stuff happens. We're the insurance you hope you never have to use but love when you do need it. If something has to go wrong, it's better to have it happen before the show rather than during it. We were prepared to fix any problems we encountered, but we weren't prepared for what happened.

If the sound check went well, we were essentially done with our part of the job. After hours of work we were looking forward to some sit-down time because when the show was over, we had to clean everything up. Just when we thought we were almost done the musician's AV tech came to ask us about the audio cables we'd run. We were using standard, everyday XLR cables. If you don't know what those are, think of them as a typical extension cord except that they carry audio instead of electricity. For what we were doing, nothing but an XLR would work, and one cable was no different from another aside from them varying in length.

For some reason this tech had gotten in his head that some cables had been "pre-set" for the show. There are no settings on a cable; it just carries the signal from A to B, so our first thought was that he meant that the sound board had been or needed to be pre-set in some way. No, it wasn't the sound board, we were supposed to be using the "pre-set" cables.

We tried explaining to him that all of our cables were exactly the same. He wasn't convinced. What do you do when someone wants you to give him a flat-tailed barktopus? If he won't take "that doesn't exist" for an answer, and he won't leave you alone until you come up with one, you have to present some kind of solution. We had to figure out what he really wanted or come up with some way to satisfy him.

Those of us running the sound check asked the supervisors and managers if they had any idea what this guy was asking for. They didn't, and we came to regret asking the question. One person in the chain of command took the idea of "the customer is always right" to the extreme. If a client said to bark like a dog, we were to ask if they had a preference on the breed we should imitate. His solution was to have us rerun all of the XLR cables. That would require unhooking everything, pulling up a lot of painstakingly secured cables, laying down several yards of new cable which had to be done to the hotel standard of perfectly straight lines, and carefully securing it all again for the sake of safety. That was a lot of work the first time when the atrium was empty; now we would have to work around all the people getting ready for the show. And, of course, we still had to perform the sound check.

We not only had no intention of doing that much unnecessary work, but we also weren't confident that we could accomplish all of it in the amount of time we had. If it'd been a matter of changing a few connections we'd have no trouble. Tape was the problem. We used rolls of heavy tape to cover each cable in two overlapping strips. This held everything down flat against the carpet which prevented tripping hazards and protected our equipment. For the sake of aesthetics and safety, we were expected to have straight and even lines meaning that we had to be precise and thorough, which is almost impossible to do quickly in a room that size full of bustling people who aren't paying attention to where they're stepping.

With the exception of our supervisor who had other responsibilities at that moment, we were the hotel's best and brightest. If we couldn't get it done, we had nobody on which we could call to jump in like some audio tech superhero to save the day with superhuman speed. So, we quickly devised a cunning plan.

We made a big show of pulling up and replacing one section of the existing cable. With the first section done, we split off to take care of different portions. We each carried enough equipment to make it look like we were rewiring the entire hotel. We made sure to look like we were grabbing for the stuff we were carrying while trying to look slightly frantic. What we were actually doing was carefully pulling up the safety tape just enough to make it look like we were removing it, then setting it back down without actually changing anything at all.

The show went off without a hitch and nobody said another word about "pre-set" cables. As far as I know, our "customer is always right" boss never knew how we pulled the wool over his eyes, nor did he complement our lightning quick speed.

Another of my favorite laugh-out-loud moments came from a guy serving as someone's tech. This person had come with a group as their full-time tech advisor. I don't know if that was his job all the time, but that was his capacity while they were at our hotel. He called for assistance with his projector, so I headed to his meeting room. After studying his setup for a few minutes, I located a solution that I overlooked at first because it was so simple: he hadn't turned on the power to the projector. I showed him where the power switch was located. Under his breath he repeated, "power switch, power switch, power switch" like he was afraid he was going to forget it. And he was being paid for his technical knowledge? At least he was appreciative and not one to be arrogant in his ignorance.

I tried not to make assumptions about anyone before I met them. Sometimes, as with the tech advisor, people knew less than I thought they should while others, like a man who was dressed like he was headed to a rodeo after his meeting, didn't need any help at all, even with equipment that most clients preferred us to handle. Everything I thought I'd learned vanished when I heard, "Chad, I need to warn you about the group coming in."

I began hearing, and not for the first time, horror stories about Catholic priests being difficult and demanding - expecting people to do more work for less money because of who they were or making a stink whenever something wasn't to their liking, even if they were the ones at fault. To be fair, I've heard horror stories about Protestant pastors as well, but I have less personal experience with Catholics. While I now have family members who are nuns and enjoy hanging out at a local monastery, I had at that point never met any Catholic clergy face to face. I was to be the primary point of contact for the technical needs of a group of priests using several of our rooms during a week-long conference.

I introduced myself to the priest in charge with dread churning sourly in my stomach. As much as I was worried about how they would treat me, I was also worried about making a social gaff. Was I supposed to address them as "Father"? In Protestant circles we use "Brother" or "Pastor" but never "Father." I wasn't comfortable with using the title, but at the same time I didn't want to offend them by being improper.

I wasn't conscious of my solution; I did it without thinking. I specifically chose wording that prevented me from having to address any of them using their title. Since they never complained, I guess they didn't mind. It worked so well that it became a pattern of mine even when I didn't realize I was doing it.

Just because my initial meeting went well didn't mean I felt at ease. It was only a matter of time before they made some ridiculous demand or yelled at me for something that was their fault. Except that didn't happen. When I spoke to the priest in charge again at the end of the day, he heaped praise and gratitude upon me.

The next day the priest was, if anything, even more appreciative of the efforts we were making to take care of his group. I started worrying that they weren't using us enough. Would they later complain we hadn't fixed problems we never knew about? I took extra care to make sure they had everything they needed. That resulted in the priest making me feel like a rock star with his praise.

By the time the event ended, I hated to see them leave. Not only were they not the nightmare I'd been warned to expect, but they were actually one of the best groups of people I ever worked with there. Friendly, pleasant, and showing the love of God in every interaction, they were one of the few groups to ever tip me, and it was the second highest tip I ever got at that job.

The best tipper I ever had went the extra mile. They were a client running an extended event at the hotel, and they had so much of our equipment for so long that I was assigned to them and them alone. I would help out elsewhere if I had free time, but as far as I was concerned, they were the only client we had. I was more than their point of contact; I was their right hand. I saw almost as much of them during that time as I did my regular coworkers.

As with the priests, they appreciated the efforts we took to make sure they had everything they needed. Not only did they leave me with the single biggest tip I've ever gotten at any job, when they found out I was working for them on my birthday they surprised me with a cake. I still use the plate that cake came on in my kitchen.

Most of our clients weren't so gracious as to tip me, but none were bad enough to generate a story to tell (although I wouldn't presume to say that was the case for everyone on the team). In my experience, even when clients weren't happy that the giant screen they were promised wouldn't fit in the tiny room they were renting, most of them could see reason. That wasn't always the case with the salespeople.

I don't know if they received a lower commission when we weren't able to provide the high-dollar items they had rented or if they thought it made them look bad in the eyes of the clients, but they would get furious with us when we couldn't meet their every demand, sometime arguing with us as if they thought we were trying to hurt them in some personal way. The repeat offenders seemed to take "that's not physically possible" to mean "we don't want to do it."

As far as the individual AV staff was concerned, we didn't make any more or less money no matter what we provided to the clients. What did we care if we were renting someone a larger screen as opposed to a smaller one? The department as a whole, though, benefited from renting the higher-priced equipment so at least as far as management was concerned, the more income we could generate the better. I'm not sure why anyone would think we'd downgrade if we didn't have a reason.

I don't want to make it sound like everyone on the sales team was like this, but the recurring conflicts with certain members of the team caused me to see them as adversaries. Those that fought with us wound up causing strife with the hotel management, who would defend the sales team without question while treating the AV department as if we were doing something wrong for not being able to bend the laws of physics. I may be speaking out of turn here since I didn't work directly with the books, but I believe we were one of the most profitable departments in the entire hotel, and yet we were always treated like we were the unwanted but unavoidable relative.

The sales team weren't the only ones that caused us trouble. We had some drama in the AV department, too.

Most of the AV team was working for the hotel when I was hired, and some were still there when I left. Two (that I know of) went on to manage AV departments at that hotel and at other properties. But we did have a few other techs come and go during my time. Victor (I'll call him that because there's a Victor Hugo novel sitting beside me) was the kind of guy every good employer hopes to avoid.

Vic was a beefy and energetic guy. He was the type to say something like "Hey, little man, let me lift that heavy TV" to me, which might have been fine even though I was perfectly capable of lifting the TV myself, if his attitude had been more "I want to help" instead of "look how much stronger I am than you." He was arrogant, pushy, and not good at his job.

He wasn't there long before we all wanted him gone, but when management tried to fire him, he claimed racial discrimination and kept his job. Never mind that the human resources lady dealing with him and other members of our AV team were of the same race, nor the fact that the hotel as a whole employed a multicultural staff many of whom didn't even speak English as their first language, his threat to sue based on discrimination was enough to save him... at least for a while.

One evening, Vic was working the night shift. He was left on his own because there wasn't much to do. When the last meetings of the day ended, it was his job to collect the equipment and set up the rooms that would be holding meetings the next morning. It was maybe an hour's worth of work at a leisurely pace with nothing heavy or complicated involved. He could essentially hang out and do nothing for the majority of his shift until the rooms were available, do the work (which could've been spread out over a period of time if he didn't feel like doing everything at once), then go home. It was just about as easy a shift as an AV tech could hope to have and still have enough work to require someone be there to do it.

My job as the morning tech was to hook up any high-theft items that had to be locked away overnight (a couple of projectors in this case) and, as meeting time approached, reach out to the clients to be sure they had everything they needed. The goal on such a day was to have as little work as possible for the morning tech so that we could focus on taking care of the client, deal with any unforeseen problems, and start working on the events taking place later in the day. I also intended to check the quality of Vic's work, because I didn't trust him to do a good job. I gave myself some extra time in case I had to redo anything, which is the only reason a pressing situation didn't become a complete disaster.

Vic should have gone home hours before I arrived, so I was shocked and concerned to see him still sitting in the office when I walked in. Unless something had gone horribly wrong there was no reason for him to be there. "Is everything OK?" I asked him.

"Yeah, it's good," he replied. I shrugged. Since there seemed to be no emergency, I decided to go take care of my morning rounds then come back to find out more about why he was still there. Within a couple of minutes, I was back and approaching panic mode.

"Did you not set up the meetings for this morning?"

"Oh, uh, no I didn't get around to that."

"Did you break down the meetings from yesterday?"

"No."

"What did you do all night? Why are you still here?"

He didn't have an answer for me, and I didn't have time

to press the issue. Those meetings had to be ready within the hour, and while the equipment from the day before was less vital, it would be in the way if other departments needed those rooms for other meetings.

I knew that I could do a faster room setup than Vic could and would be better off if he wasn't in the way. I told him I would set up the morning meetings if he would break down yesterday's rooms. Questions and blame could wait until the clients were taken care of.

I piled up two carts with everything I would need for all the meetings without having to waste time on trips back to the office. I must have looked like a junk peddler pushing one cart while pulling the other both full of projectors, cords, wires, screens, and whatever else I needed.

I had all the rooms set up in record time. I was breathing hard by the time I got back to the office, which was one part exertion and one part anger. It was time to figure out what was going on with Vic, except that I couldn't find him. With suspicion solidifying into certainty, I looked at the paperwork to see that instead of doing the work I'd told him to do, he'd left to go home. I spent the rest of the morning doing the work that Vic should have been doing the night before in addition to my normal responsibilities.

I wonder if Vic would've done this no matter which one of us was the morning tech, or if he targeted me specifically because he thought I wouldn't fight back. Either way, I made sure it was a decision he would regret. By the time our supervisor arrived, I had a detailed mental checklist of infractions ready to deliver.

I wasn't there when the supervisor confronted Vic, so the following is nothing more than my impression of how the meeting went: "I have you on multiple fireable offenses. Do you want to walk with me down to HR, or do you want to hand in your notice?" Vic opted to quit and we never had to deal with him again. I never take joy in getting someone into trouble. In most cases, I'd rather cover for you than tell on you. In Vic's case, I left out no detail to ensure that we could be rid of him.

I left the hotel to take a job closer to home, one that paid a good bit more. I stayed there for a few years before I moved south of Atlanta to take the job I've been working ever since. Having gone through a divorce and trying to get my finances in better shape after taking Dave Ramsey's *Financial Peace University* course, I began considering what I might be able to do to make some extra cash. I thought I remembered my hotel supervisor living somewhere in my general area and discovered that he actually lived only a few miles away. Even better, he now managed a different location for the same hotel chain, and that location wasn't very far from where we lived. I asked what he thought about hiring me on a freelance basis, and a few weeks later I was handling a lot of his weekend workload.

It was probably the easiest job I've ever had. It was much like my previous stint with the hotel chain except that since I wasn't an actual employee, I got to bypass most of their regular demands. The majority of my job consisted of babysitting meetings and making sure that rooms were cleaned up or set up for the following day. Since I had to be on hand in case a client needed me, but I couldn't do anything with the rooms that were being used, I spent a lot of my time reading books while I monitored the radio for calls. Then I did the single dumbest thing I've ever done at a job.

My downfall was that my schedule was sporadic. I'd work a Saturday here and a Sunday there. One weekend, I forgot that I'd agreed to work and failed to show up. It was an honest mistake that I should've been more careful not to make. It was the end of my freelance hotel work.

I called my friend in a panic the next day, worried that I had left him with some disaster on his hands. Fortunately, it wasn't anything he couldn't handle, although it did mean he couldn't use me anymore. I understood. It was my own fault.

It turned out to be less of a loss than it first seemed to be, because not long after that the hotel decided that they didn't want an in-house AV team, they wanted to use an outside company. Despite the years of dedicated work my supervisor had given the hotel chain, and his proven track record of turning a profit for them, they unceremoniously dropped him like a bag of moldy tangerines.

My freelance no-show was probably enough to ensure that the hotel would never want me back, but the way they treated the AV staff makes me unwilling to trust them enough to ever work for them again. I never felt like they had any real love or loyalty towards us, but now I see that the truth was more horrifying than I would've ever imagined. "Thanks for your many years of hard work or whatever. Be off the property in five minutes or we'll call security." That may not have been their words to my friend, but it might as well have been.

Even though the end of the story isn't a happy one, I feel like I did well at the hotel. Even when arrogant coworkers and greedy salespeople were making life difficult, I was at my best when dealing with people - quite a contrast to my days as a bumbling salesman. I think the reason is the same as why I was able to outsell other stores when it came to computers in my college retail job: I was comfortable with the technology. I didn't have to sell anything at the hotel, only make sure that everything worked. In a different application of the concept, that's a lot like what I'd be doing when I finally locked down a true career.

I still didn't yet know that I was on the autism spectrum. Nor did I understand all the reasons why I had more success with this job than others before it. I didn't see how much my previous experience had prepared me for the hotel or how much that job prepared me for what was coming next. However, whether I realized it or not, I was finally learning to play to my strengths rather than jumping on the first idealistic dream that came my way with the blind hope that it would turn out better than my current situation.

The hotel wasn't my dream job; it could be aggravating and demanding but considering what I'd endured - a job that pushed me until I got sick, one that blamed me for other people's choices, and one that had cult-like control over every aspect of my life - it lifted my spirits and boosted my confidence. I was, for the first time since college, both good at my job and liking what I was doing. I no longer had a clear career plan, so I might not have left the hotel at all if I hadn't been going to another job with higher pay and a much shorter commute, but one benefit of a good job, even if it isn't exactly what we're hoping for, is that it provides freedom to explore what else life has to offer instead of being pushed from one bad situation to another. I may not ever want to return to working in hotel AV, but I couldn't have gotten to where I am now without it.

11

I.T. Chicken

Ever been in a chicken plant? Is it strange that I would leave hotel audio/video to work at one? This company handled birds from the egg to the plate and showed me sights I never expected to see. I saw the newborns - crates full of dozens of fluffy, newly hatched chicks, I saw conveyors hauling an endless line of birds ready to be processed and packaged, and I saw trucks hauling the live and processed animals back and forth. About the only part I didn't actually witness with my own eyes was the slaughter, but I sure smelled it.

That slaughter plant was my least favorite place to go. It's probably one of those smells you get acclimated to after a while, but every time I pulled into the parking lot, I got a disgusting slap in the face. Ever walk past a dumpster behind a restaurant on a hot day? It was a lot like that, except that the smell was everywhere all the time.

I was part of the Information Technology or "IT" team. We made sure that all of the computers ran like they should, which included office desktops as well as the simple data entry terminals in the plants as well as anything connected to them: monitors, keyboards, etc. I eventually oversaw all of the printers, which meant troubleshooting, installation, maintenance - virtually anything you need to do with a printer (the scene of the printer's death in the movie *Office Space* is quite cathartic to me).

We never had to get up close and personal with any of the birds nor did we work on any of the machines that handled them, but some of the equipment we maintained had us all but nose-to-nose with that stuff. Our team went almost everywhere there was to go in the company because virtually no one did their job without some sort of computer technology, even if it was just tracking inventory and printing labels. I doubt anyone else at the company saw the inside of every single building (close to a dozen spread out over a handful of cities if my memory is accurate) on a regular basis like we did. I guess that can make a job interesting or annoying, depending on how you view things.

I actually kind of enjoyed walking through some of the processing plants. Since we were dealing with raw meat that had to meet strict FDA guidelines, the plants had to be kept cold. I like the cold. A lot of them stayed wet, too. And they were never very bright. I could almost imagine walking through some damp cave when I was passing through those areas.

It was fascinating, if gruesome, to see the machines that handled the meat. It was like seeing robots getting dinner ready to go into the oven. I love chicken: fried, grilled, on a Chick-Fil-A biscuit, on a McDonald's biscuit, on a Bojangles biscuit... OK, you get the idea. So, if anything, the packaging plants made me hungry. As disgusting as the slaughterhouses smelled, that was never enough to put me off eating birds.

Some of the meat was packaged raw and sold to other companies (I discovered that I'd been eating chicken from the company for years, I just never knew it because it was sold under a different brand name). Some of it was processed for our own label. One of my favorite perks of visiting one particular plant was getting to taste some of the new recipe experiments. We rarely went there without getting fed - not a meal's worth but certainly a nice snack, and almost always very tasty.

I'd had a long road from broadcasting to IT, and not much of it involved preparing me for a job with computers. I don't think I could've handled it if I hadn't been a gamer. I knew all about computer specifications, replacing hard drives, upgrading memory, and increasing my processing power thanks to being motivated to play games like *Star Wars: Jedi Knight*. If you are familiar with the series, you might be asking, "Which one?" The answer is "all of them."

Thanks to those interests, I knew something about what I would be doing as an IT tech, but when it came to detailed knowledge of servers, the more complicated workings of Windows, and computer hardware beyond what applied to my gaming I was behind everyone else on the staff. I think it was more my connections than my qualifications that got me into that job, a fact which I'm not sure my boss was ever especially happy about.

I won't say my boss mistreated me, it was never that severe (certainly nothing like what I endured at the textile plant), but she had little patience where I was concerned. After joining the team, I was put through a training course for the software we used. That's what I did for eight hours a day for the first couple of weeks. One day, after staring at a computer screen for hours, having stared at it for hours the previous day and the day before that, I got up to stretch and look out a window to give my eyes a break. I commented on something I saw out there and was quickly and firmly instructed to get back to my training. At the time, I felt it was strict but probably no more so than what was expected of everyone else. Looking back on it after everything else that happened, I'm not so sure that was the case.

On the surface all appeared to be fine for the first few months. Everyone in the IT office got along pretty well. I felt like some of them looked down on me for being the least trained and experienced of the team, but I never felt like anyone disliked me. I assumed that eventually I would be a full-fledged member of the team and even thought I was carving out a niche for myself as the printer expert when I started taking that as my primary focus.

I began seeing my boss in a different light after a visit to one of our plants where I was checking and cleaning the printers. Someone grabbed me to ask me about an issue she was having with her computer running slowly. In an attempt to be proactive and helpful rather than giving her an "I don't know, go away" kind of answer, but also knowing that I had to get to my next task, I suggested she could run a defrag (a program for optimizing a computer's hard drive). The hard drives in those computers were small, so the amount of time it would take to defragment any one of them would be minimal. I figured if it helped at all that would keep the user happy until we could take a closer look at any more significant problems, and if it didn't help it also wouldn't do any harm.

When I returned to the IT office, I didn't even have the chance to mention the problem to anyone before my boss was asking why I had told the user to defragment her hard drive. Amidst me trying to explain myself, I was informed that the user had already talked to one of our other techs who'd already told her to run the defrag. Of course, the user hadn't told me she'd spoken to anyone nor that she had already done anything with the computer.

I learned two things from that interaction. First, at least as far as my relationship with the boss went, taking initiative would be frowned upon. The whole reason I did what I did was because I thought it would show my boss that I was trying to step out beyond expectations, helping our users instead of brushing them off. It wouldn't be the last time putting forth some extra effort at this job got me nothing positive in return.

Second, never assume you're the first or only person a user has talked to about a problem, because they would rather give you the least amount of information possible than to volunteer what you need to know to make a fully informed decision about what to do next. I'd given the user the exact same instruction that our more senior tech had, but in my case, it was a bad thing for no other reason than because I didn't know that the user had already spoken to someone. Users tend to get annoyed with techs asking too many questions or trying elementary solutions to problems, but we do that because of people like this who willfully withhold information that comes back to bite us.

Probably my most draining moment as far as any motivation to go beyond the bare minimum of my job requirements was when I designed a relatively sophisticated printer database for the company. That was a big endeavor for me because I am not and have never been a programmer. I was proud of what I was able to accomplish and had high hopes that it would make a good impression on bosses and coworkers alike. I didn't get the response for which I'd hoped.

In my job of overseeing the printers, I had a regular rotation of plants and offices at which I would clean and maintain everything they had except for those with a maintenance contract (usually the huge scanner/printers that required rooms of their own). I quickly discovered that we didn't have good records on which printers were at which locations or what we had in our office storeroom.

During my first couple of weeks as Print Master, I lost track of a printer. Did one of the other techs grab it? Did I accidentally use it at a location that was supposed to get a different device? Did someone throw it out thinking that it wasn't working? Was it stolen?

The missing printer bothered me partly because I don't like losing track of things and partly because the way things were going at this job, I was concerned that I'd be blamed for the loss. When a second printer went missing a few weeks later I feared being suspected as a thief. I knew I had to find a better way to keep up with our inventory.

My inspiration for a solution came from playing around with Microsoft: Access to create a database that could track my CD collection. My time as a DJ resulted in me having a large music library, with several rare promotional and pre-release albums containing tracks not found in stores plus interview clips and promos that I'd produced myself. I knew my library well, but that's a lot to remember particularly if a situation or request called for something I didn't play often.

My solution was a database I could tailor to whatever need I had. It might not be impressive now compared to what some of our modern apps can do, but for an amateur attempt it wasn't bad. I could list individual tracks for every album I owned with tags for situations in which I might want to use them (such as marking Christmas songs or ones that would be good for a Halloween party). I could view the data for any track, album, or artist and go from one to the other with the click of a button. If I wanted to know every single song that I might want to use at a birthday party, for example, I could generate a full list in seconds. I couldn't take my database with me to most jobs (we didn't yet have cloud storage and portable internet), but I could plan my night ahead of time and print lists to take with me.

I decided to apply that idea to my job of taking care of our printers. I taught myself how to use Access beyond anything I'd attempted before, which required plenty of off-the-clock studying at home. I went through every manual we had at the office, some of them quite lengthy, and practiced by modifying my music database and creating new ones. By the time I was done I had databases for all of my books, comic books, and DVDs.

When the database was finished, I could call up an exact count of every make and model of every printer we owned. I could tell you where each one was physically, when it was due for maintenance, and what (if any) troubles I'd encountered with it. If I needed to swap one machine for another, I could update the records in a matter of minutes with notes on what I needed to do next to either one of them. If a printer was removed from use, I knew exactly which one it was and exactly why. Never again would the wrong printer be put in the wrong location without me being able to find it.

I was pleased with my creation, and I can honestly say that from the time I implemented my database to the time I left I never once lost track of another printer. It might not have been perfect in every way, but it proved to be useful enough that the company continued using it after I left (which I know because they called me at my new job to ask me questions about it).

My qualm was that while I was the Print Master, I didn't have sole control over every device. If one of the other techs needed to swap out a printer somewhere, it was neither possible nor beneficial to stop them. So, I needed them to update the database if they made any changes. They could also leave me notes if they ran into any issues I needed to look at during my next round of maintenance or if I needed to replace a part. To this end, I needed them to be able to edit the records or to give me the information so that I could. I gave them all a crash course in how to operate the database with an open invitation to come to me for help with it. I didn't think it would be difficult for a computer savvy group.

Most of my coworkers never expressed any difficulty with using my database. The praise they gave me for my efforts made me feel good about what I'd accomplished. One coworker, though, couldn't seem to grasp the flow of data. I don't remember now the exact details of what caused the confusion, but it boiled down to the proper procedure for updating the information.

The basic logic was similar to this: if Records A, B, and C all referenced List 1 and something in that list needed to be updated then you made the edit in List 1, not the Records. If you made the edit in Record A, it would apply only to that specific one so that Records B and C still showed the old information. If you made the edit to List 1, it would apply to Records A, B, and C.

Think of it like electronic menus at a restaurant. You can (hypothetically speaking) edit each of the menus if you want to, but they all pull their information from a computer in the office. The price of one of the menu items has changed and needs to be updated on all three menus. Which makes more sense, to update each menu or to update the computer in the office so that it tells all three menus what the new price is?

This one particular coworker would make the edit to the menu (or the Record) rather than the computer in the office (or the List) which meant that everything else now had incorrect data, requiring extra work to fix it on my part. No amount of me explaining the proper way to do it could get this person to do it correctly.

This eventually became enough of a problem that it escalated to our boss. The boss, who never once gave me a pat on the back for my efforts, told me that it was my fault for not designing an easier to use database rather than the fault of the person not using it correctly. Never mind that nobody else had trouble with it, nor that the coworker had the option of telling me what needed to be changed so that I could do it right instead of going behind her to clean up the mess she made. Rather than tell the other person she should use the database according to my instructions, our boss told me that I should've create a better database.

I felt like my boss viewed my creation as garbage. Added to the frustration of the coworker's blatant refusal to follow instructions, I began to worry that everyone else in the office thought I'd created a silly bit of junk and were just being too nice to say it to my face. I knew I'd created something useful because it helped me do my job better on a daily basis, but from then on, I quietly fixed the data problems without expecting anyone to care enough to try to do it right. That was the last time I attempted to do anything for that company outside the bare minimum of my job requirements.

Taking initiative got me in trouble. Going above and beyond gained me nothing but criticism. But the biggest insult I endured came from how I handled social interaction. I wasn't happy with my job once I felt like nothing I did would be good enough for them, but this was the encounter that put me onto the path of finding new employment.

All of us in the department worked a typical eight-hour shift plus another half hour for lunch. There were on-call and emergency situations that went beyond that, but those weren't at all an everyday or even every week occurrence.

In addition to that, a couple of us traded off backup duty. Every day someone had to stay late to run a backup of all the computer systems. Periodically, additional backups were required (a monthly in addition to the daily, for example) requiring us to stay even later. These had to be labeled and taken to a separate building where they were stored in a vault. This all took time that was beyond our standard eight hours. To compensate, when it wasn't our week to run the backups, those of us on the rotation got to go home a little early.

Even when I wasn't happy with members of the team over the frustrations with the database, we were still friendly with each other. Three of us were close to the same age and all nerds, so we actually hung out together quite a bit outside of work. We had gaming parties, had shared interests in movies and music (one of them was responsible for getting me hooked on "Stargate: SG-1" which became one of my all-time favorite TV shows), and visited each other's houses. However, I also had a life outside of my work friends. I was recently married and bought a house during my time there, and I was active in my church as one of our leading sound engineers, so I spent a lot of time helping with services, band practices, and events.

As an autistic introvert, I hit my social interaction max capacity a lot faster than most people. Not all auties are introverts. I think we're often mistaken for such because of how challenging socializing can be for us. A lot of factors play into how we deal with interactions in general and on a case-by-case basis. I used to consider myself anti-social because I can and have existed with a minimum of human interaction. I make a conscious decision to not isolate myself because I love my family and because I believe that our choices in life have eternal ramifications which pushes me to want to help others.

When dealing with people I don't know, I find it easier if I'm acting in an official capacity. As the service director at my church, for example, I'm not shy about approaching a guest speaker to ensure I get what I need for our cameras. I may need them to stand more towards the center of the stage or make sure we have the best angle possible on an object or gesture they want the audience to see. Part of my job is making sure the cameras see what they need to. Doing my job gives me a confidence I don't necessarily have otherwise.

When I'm not doing a job, just another face in the crowd, I find public speaking easier than one-on-one interaction. People tell me all the time that they don't know how I can get up in front of a crowd. I'm the opposite; I don't know how they talk privately with a person they don't know with such ease.

Not everyone, autie or not, can do what I do, just like there are jobs for which I'm not well suited. If we were all the same, the world would be a boring place. It's up to each individual to figure out their own strengths and weaknesses. What makes them uneasy? What helps them cope?

If I'm in a large crowd, I do best if I can keep to myself

(or with a small group of friends) or focus on a single conversation. If I can't do that, you'll more often than not see me sitting quietly or finding a place to go where I'm not surrounded by everyone else. I've learned to disengage for a little while if I need to gather myself instead of trying to force myself to interact just because I've convinced myself that it's what everyone else expects. I usually have my wife or a friend with me who makes sure I feel comfortable taking the time I need, rather than letting the stress continue to build.

In an environment like my IT job or a family gathering, I don't have to worry about crowds so much, but being around people tires me even if I'm having a good time. Disengaging helps with that, too. Finding a quiet spot or a solitary focus helps recharge my social batteries so that I can keep going. Having some time at the end of the day to watch a little TV or read a book is like taking medicine. If I go too many days without time to read, my stress level rises…especially if I'm around people a lot. Learning to carve out those solitary times has made my life happier and more productive.

While auties are not always introverted, most if not all of us deal with sensory overload. That's one of the most common defining traits of autism. Too much noise, certain types of noise (typically worsened by misophonia - see the appendices at the end of the book for more information on what misophonia is), touching, lights, and odors are some of the most common contributing factors to sensory overload. Everyone has odors they find revolting, boundaries on who can touch them and when, lights that bother them, and so on. Auties are often more sensitive to these sensations, with more severe reactions to what we find unpleasant. I personally am more sensitive to sounds than anything else. I can become tense, stressed, and irritable over unpleasant sounds with the most extreme cases causing me to (unintentionally) harm myself.

Two things help with my sensory overload: control and removal. I try to control my sensory input with music. Depending on the situation, I don't necessarily have to drown out all other noise as long as I can mentally latch on to music I like and focus on it.

Sometimes, though, I have to remove myself from the source of the overload. I've been known to physically walk away as I attempt to escape whatever is bothering me, but leaving isn't always possible or necessary; I can "remove" myself by shutting out everything around me. My favorite method of removal by shut-out is putting a sonic wall of loud guitars between me and the cause of my stress. My wife has been known to tell me, "You need to listen to some Galactic Cowboys and calm down." I have a playlist of my heaviest metal music which I call my "Bad Day Remedy." I can access it anywhere at any time, although unless I'm at home or in my car it's only useful if I have headphones. I don't listen to it only when I'm having a bad day, but it's better than a drug for calming me down, especially if the source of the aggravation is coming from any sort of sensory stimulation.

Headphones and music have been an integral part of my life since I was young, long before I understood how much that helped me or why. I'm more sociable now than I was as a teen because I've learned healthy ways to handle situations, but if I'm around people for an extended period of time you'll still frequently find me reading a book with my music playing.

In an IT job situation like the chicken plant, I usually didn't have the option of music or of stepping away to gather myself. Since I didn't yet know I was on the autism spectrum, I didn't always understand why I was reacting the way I was nor how to deal with it effectively. I knew music helped me cope, I just didn't know exactly why.

After a full day of work with coworkers, I typically had all of the social interaction I could handle. Friends or not, I was ready for a break by the time my shift was done. I needed isolation and sensory control - needed it so badly I could hardly wait to get to my car at the end of the day.

At my current job, I work in an office that holds considerably more people, but I don't have to interact with them all day every day. I spend most of my day on my computer doing my solitary software testing or document creation. That's taught me that there's a huge difference in being around people and having to constantly interact with them. The latter is what I had to do at the chicken plant.

My boss and I were having a conversation about my job performance after I'd been there for a while. She pointed out how everyone else, when it was time for them to go home on their early days (meaning that the rest of the team would still be working rather than all of us leaving together), would hang around the office talking with those of us still on the clock, sometimes for as long as half an hour. My desire to actually go home when my shift ended rather than stand at the door and chit chat counted as a mark against me.

I've never in my working life been reprimanded for a more absurd reason than not wanting to spend extra time socializing with my coworkers with whom I had, more likely than not on any given day, spent the vast majority of the past eight hours (plus lunch which we always took together because we were fed for free by our outstanding company cafeteria) instead of going home at the end of my shift. If my boss didn't know that some of us hung out over the weekends, she didn't pay much attention to our in-office conversations, but that should've had no bearing at all on her view of my work performance.

Leaving that job was the best thing for me for any number of reasons (not the least of which was me becoming a leader in the field of software testing rather than fighting to catch up with the rest of the IT team), but this previously unspoken expectation of regular off-the-clock socializing was a significant factor in my desire to find other employment. I've never been expected to stay after hours to chat even though I like many of my current coworkers enough that we've been known to get together for meals, games, and movies outside of work.

Don't think I have only complaints about my life at the chicken plant. I do miss my friends there, and I don't think I would've been offered a job with my current company if not for my IT experience so for that I will be forever grateful. They also made it possible for me to earn my second college degree, this time in computer science. I'd say that a little aggravation over unreasonable social expectations was worth it when I consider the big picture.

I'll close this chapter with my favorite insane helpdesk support story.

For our office work we used Windows, but many of the data entry terminals in the various plants were too simple to support a graphic user interface. For those tasks we used a text-based interface similar to DOS. That means there were no images, just words. To do anything within the system, you had to know the proper commands to type in and when to enter them.

One of our users called me up at the end of the workday. (Don't these kinds of things always happen at the end of the day?) It was my late week, so everyone else had gone home while I waited until time to run the backup. My heart sank when the phone rang because that meant my long day was most likely about to get longer, especially if I had to drive over to one of the other buildings to fix a problem.

The user on the phone was a lady I knew. I'd always considered her to be a little smarter than our average user partly because she'd been in her position for a while and knew how to do her job. I had some hope that this might turn out to be a relatively easy call.

The system had given her an error. To figure out what to do about that, I needed to know if there was a blank line following the text because that would mean the system was expecting a command.

I asked the user, "Is there a line after the error?"

"I don't know," she said.

"A line, a blank line at the end of the text."

"I don't know."

"Could you go to the screen?"

"It's right here in front of me."

"Can you read me the error again?" She did. "Is there anything else on the screen?"

"I don't have a fancy computer degree. I don't know about that stuff."

If there's anything I learned from working in a helpdesk capacity, it's that if people make up their minds that they don't know anything about computers, it causes them to act completely helpless if they have to do anything more than type something familiar on a keyboard or click on an image. I've come up with a few possible explanations for this. I think some of them genuinely convince themselves that they don't know enough to do anything, therefore they don't bother to try. Others, I think, develop a stubborn laziness that causes them to do as little as possible, even going as far as to refuse to learn or to deliberately give incorrect information to anyone trying to help them, hoping the "computer whiz" will get frustrated enough to take over and do everything themselves. These types think you're being belligerent when you have them reboot (which really does fix a great many issues) or check to be sure cords are plugged in (I learned the hard way to never assume that they are or that the user has checked them). In the most extreme cases, they claim that they can't answer a question that any average kindergartner who knows their shapes could.

How many ways can you describe a simple, flat, blank line to a typically functional adult? I didn't expect her to know what to do with that line, I just needed to know whether or not the line existed. At first, I thought the user was misunderstanding me which is why I tried so many times to clarify what I was asking. Finally, I decided that she would rather force me to drive over to her location (when I should be getting ready to go home for the day) rather than give me the small bit of information I needed to solve the problem immediately on the phone.

Frustrated and on the verge of losing my patience, I decided to take a chance and give her a command to type. It solved the problem, which meant that she did have the line I was asking about. There's no way she couldn't have seen it, she just didn't want to tell me it was there. If you ever work a computer helpdesk job, you can expect that and worse out of users.

I've read that the three biggest stressors in life are

changing jobs, moving, and getting a divorce. I did all three at the same time. At least I got them all out of the way. When my soon-to-be ex-wife and I decided to part ways, we put our house on the market. During this time, I interviewed for my next job. When we knew the sale of the house would go through, I turned in my notice at the chicken plant and made plans to move to a new town with my cat Escher.

Whatever complaints I may have about that job, they threw me a nice going away party. The chefs in the kitchen gave me a hot pepper plant, and the IT department gave me a nice pen which I still use whenever I write my story ideas on paper. I had some interesting experiences there and got to know some great people. I now work at a place that appreciates me more, which makes a huge impact on my motivation to do more for them. I don't know how I'd respond now to someone telling me I don't spend enough of my free time socializing with coworkers instead of going home at the end of my shift, but I do know that with an autie like me that sort of an expectation isn't going to generate a more positive work environment.

12

Code Breaker

I'm going to depart from the insane work experiences to tell you about my biggest success. This is where the road has taken me.

My IT experience helped me land a software support job which was, in a lot of ways, similar to the helpdesk portion of my previous work. Here, though, instead of keeping chicken processing plants running I was helping home health and hospice agencies take care of their patients. In a sense, I went from dealing with death to life.

I barely knew what hospice was at my first interview, and I definitely couldn't have told you what an RN, LPN, PT, or OT was. I'd never heard of an ICD-9 code (we don't use those anymore) and didn't know an OASIS assessment from a HIPOC.

Fortunately, the company was more interested in my technical abilities than my healthcare knowledge.

We don't do this anymore, but in those days the interview process was the most bizarre I've ever encountered. I got interviewed by every person on the team, with each of them having the chance to veto my hiring. I would later get the chance to do the same for other applicants.

I was given a selection of technical and logic puzzles to solve. For one of those, a physical, store-bought puzzle ("Traffic Jam" I think was the name), I had the second fastest solution time in the history of the company. It was a challenging and fun interview. I got hired and went directly to orientation and training where nobody chastised me if I needed to stretch my legs and rest my eyes for a few minutes.

I wasn't always the best when it came to dealing with people. It wasn't that they didn't like me, in fact, most of my interactions with them were pleasant even when they were frustrated with some problem that they needed help fixing. I even developed something of a reputation thanks to my knowledge of printers. I knew more than some of our agencies' IT departments, and they always appreciated my willingness to help find solutions that eluded other techs.

I was, by all measures, a decent customer support specialist. But the more sociable among us developed a rapport with their clients that I was never able to achieve. Nobody asked for me by name (unless they were having printer trouble) or knew anything personal about me. "How's the family?" "Who are you rooting for in the next sportsball event?" Those sorts of conversations never happened with me. I was strictly a get-in-there-and-get-the-problem-solved kind of guy. There's nothing wrong with that, I suppose; I got the results our users needed, but rarely did anyone other than a coworker go to my boss to say how awesome I was. Other specialists got that and I don't mind admitting that it made me a little jealous.

Maybe that's why when the QA (quality assurance - also known as quality control at some places) testing department needed some extra help from the support team, I was asked to train with them. That was my first introduction to testing. Little did I know I would very soon be thrown to the proverbial wolves.

For different personal reasons, both of our QA testers quit a mere few weeks apart. The company was desperate. They needed a replacement from within who already knew the software as opposed to hiring a tester who knew nothing about our product, and despite my minimal training I was the best option they had. They asked me to step into the role, and my life was forever changed.

The qualities that made me a terrible salesman or got me in trouble for being too unsociable made me the ideal person to sit isolated at a desk pouring through software functionality and comparing lines of data against what had been entered into the programming code. The company originally had plans to hire a second tester to fill the other vacancy, but they never had to (which isn't to say that I never needed help, just not on a full-time basis). Within a year, I'd completely rewritten all of our testing documentation, some of which influenced our approach to testing in other departments for years to come.

I quickly developed a reputation for discovering the strangest bugs. I was worried that the programmers would hate me for finding all their flaws, but they were exactly the opposite. I was essential in making their code better, so they appreciated my efforts, which of course encouraged me to keep finding everything I could. On my side of things, I was always careful to not rub anyone's face in their mistakes.

People who are excellent in their customer support roles (which I hate doing and am not great at) have told me they don't know how I do my job. At one point, I would've said that any knowledgeable support specialist could be a QA tester, but the times I've been able to guide them through their own testing projects has proven to me that I was wrong. Being good at one doesn't mean you're good at the other. And if there is a moral to this collection of experiences, that would be it.

We're not all designed the same!

Where I failed as a salesman, I excel as a tester. Not everyone necessarily needs to be a socialite (although I sometimes wonder if the high-level executives realize that). It actually helps in my position that I don't crave interaction, because I don't go stir-crazy when I'm isolated working on a solitary project. Not only does nobody care that I'm an autistic introvert, but they actually appreciate the qualities that keep me plugging away at a job they don't want to have to do themselves. Nobody ever gives me a hard time when I don't say a single word during a meeting, but they also know that I'm available for any and every question they ever have for me.

If there's anything you can take away from reading my crazy adventures, I want it to be that you don't have to be like everyone else. I had to spend years doing jobs I didn't like before I found the one perfectly suited for me, one that I wouldn't have even considered if it hadn't been pushed upon me. Retail and fast food forced me to learn some people skills which have been a necessity everywhere else. The hotel job helped me develop the ability to aid people with their technology, which was beneficial when I transitioned to IT which, in turn, helped me get the job with the software company that gave me the training I needed to step into the tester's role.

I envy people who set their sights on a career early and can see that through. I have a cousin who's an E.R. doctor. That takes a level of long-term dedication that I admire. I wonder where I might be now if I'd had that level of dedication to writing earlier in life. I feel like I've started and stopped so many times that I haven't achieved everything I'd hoped I would. I have to take the time to see the positive that's come out of the negative and push myself towards new goals.

My dream of working in broadcasting never amounted

to much, but even that gave me technical skills that've been useful along my path. These days I'm able to use those skills at my church as one of the lead service directors. While my brothers Otis and Paul are greeting people at the door of the building making them feel welcome, Ron is taking care of people in the sanctuary, and Dennis is handling the security team. None of that is anything I want to be doing. I mix video feeds and direct camera shots. I can't wait to be in that director's chair again next Sunday, and I'm exceedingly glad that nobody expects me to be doing those other jobs instead. It's hard to feel like those years were wasted when people around the world are thankful to be able to watch our Sunday services because of the technical team I helped establish and continue to help lead.

Looking back over my experiences I can see a path - a winding, disjointed, sometimes bizarre path, but nonetheless one that got me to where I am: working a job I like and am good at and doing good for other people by serving them with my unusual set of skills. I would call that a successful life.

Where is your path taking you?

Appendix I: What is a Con?

A convention is a gathering of people sharing an interest. At these events, vendors and keynote speakers are common. They may involve a profession or some facet of industry. Fan conventions are typically called "cons." Geeks and nerds gather to celebrate fandom of many forms. They often have celebrity guests, special events, musical performances, contests, demonstrations, movie and TV show screenings, group sing-alongs - the list goes on and on. Vendors will frequently sell collectables, comic books, literature, board and card games, weapons both real and prop, unusual clothing, replicas, and any number of other items that you're not likely to find outside of a specialty shop.

Panel discussions are one of my favorite elements of a good con. Usually held in a meeting room or a ballroom, these can draw huge crowds with people willing to stand in line for hours. The high-demand ones tend to be celebrity panels at which the guest or guests of honor usually sit at a table, from which they speak to the audience. Most of the ones I've attended involve a question-and-answer session, which are excellent opportunities for fan interaction. These usually have a central microphone where fans will stand in line until their turn to ask their question. On rare occasions, the celebrities may roam the crowd with a wireless microphone taking questions directly.

Panels don't always involve celebrities, though. Sometimes they involve experts on specific topics or fans with enough knowledge to lead a group discussion. Topics covered in these can be literally anything: real science, rumors about what's coming next in an ongoing TV show, examinations of literature, how to publish a book, a particular theme in a movie or genre, a presentation of evidence for paranormal activity, a memorial for someone who's passed on, and on and on. If I listed the topic of every panel I can recall, I would nearly double the length of this book.

Some cons have a narrow focus. *Star Wars* and numerous popular shows such as *Highlander* and *Twin Peaks* have held events entirely focused on nothing other than those franchises. Comic book, animation, and fantasy cons are common.

My favorite cons are those with a multi-genre focus. At these, you'll typically see a little bit of everything. If a stormtrooper, a hobbit, Freddy Kreuger, and Carmen Sandiego are at a table sharing drinks, you're probably at a con. I've met many of my favorite *Star Wars* authors, much of the cast of *The X-Files*, comic book legend Stan Lee, and actors from some of my favorite movies at these kinds of cons. I've hugged Doug

Jones, talked martial arts with Eric Roberts, moderated panels with Victoria Price, hung out with Jess Harnell, joked around with Jon Heder, and gotten encouragement from Dean Cain. One of my favorite and most unique experiences was an impromptu lightsaber duel with Temuera Morrison of *Star Wars* fame. Not every one of these events can deliver that same level of interaction, but I could fill a book with stories of my encounters with these people and many more.

The largest and most famous of these fan conventions is San Diego's Comic-Con. One misconception that I encounter is that all conventions are Comic-Cons. Others might be similar, although few come anywhere close to the same size and scope, but most are far smaller with a narrower focus. Two that have significance to my stories are Dragon*Con and Con Nooga.

Dragon*Con is held in Atlanta, Georgia every Labor Day weekend. With attendance in the tens of thousands, this is one of, if not the biggest con in the South. This was my first con experience and one that has remained an annual event ever since. It was at Dragon*Con that I first met my wife and the members of Fans For Christ. I've made many life-long friends because of this con, and us spending time together each year has become even more important to us than the con itself.

Con Nooga is held in Chattanooga, Tennessee every year in mid-February. This one is special to me because I worked on the staff as the head of the horror track for a few years. It was here that I met George Demick and got involved with Flickering

Candle Productions' movies. Perhaps my proudest moment at this con was hosting a live commentary recording session for the movie *Deadlines,* which you can hear on the Blu-ray release. This is where I met authors like Seth Tucker and Kenyon Henry who've given me invaluable advice on writing and publishing.

If you want to experience a fan convention, I highly recommend it. You should know what you're getting yourself into before you go, though. Dragon*Con, for example, is going to have more and bigger stars than most but it'll also have the largest crowds. Finding a hotel room on site is always a challenge. A smaller event like Con Nooga may have less to offer as far as celebrity encounters but will tend to be less hectic and require less walking.

Appendix II: What is Fans For Christ?

Fans For Christ, often referred to as FFC, was founded by Steve Weese as an outreach for Christians in the world of fandom. In the early days, it was little more than an online forum and a few people behind a table at a con. It's grown to involve members from around the world. A team of volunteers leads the group with the help of a number of trusted advisors and numerous people who donate their time and money towards the success of our efforts.

FFC is one part outreach. Cons often provide fan tables where groups can interact with the attendees, usually for the promotion of an organization or cause. You might find tables for clubs, charities, musical artists, other cons, and much more. Just about any group who's willing to put the effort into maintaining a table in order to have a presence at a con can have one, depending on the events' requirements and available space.

Whenever possible, FFC gets a fan table at which we're able to set up a display that makes us visible to passersby. We try to keep at least one or two people at the table at all times, allowing con attendees to approach us. Many want to know about our beliefs. Sometimes they want prayer or to share their own journeys of faith. Not everyone is happy to see us; we certainly have plenty who judge us saying that religion has no place at a con. However, because we're inviting people to come to us rather than yelling at them from a soapbox as some do, and because we treat everyone with respect and kindness, many people who disagree with us argue in favor of our right to be there as much as any other fan. We tend to have more favorable responses than not and over the years we've been able to form strong relationships with some of the cons we attend.

We tend to be able to have discussions and engage in ministry opportunities that someone not involved with the world of fandom can't. That's because we share common ground with the fans at cons since that's who we are, too. Most of our members, including every member of the current leadership, joined because we found the FFC table at one con or another.

Many of us have written books, recorded music, or appeared in movies so we're creators as well as fans. We tend to have more fans than celebrities, but occasionally a well-known face will appear at one or another of our events. Gary Gygax was an active member near the end of his life.

FFC is also one part fellowship. We exist to encourage and pray for one another. Many life-long friendships have arisen out of the time we've spent together. I first met my wife because we were both involved with the ministry. We frequently gather for Bible studies, gaming sessions, and special events held by the cons. Whenever a con will allow, we hold a Sunday service with music and a sermon - we call it "Church at Con" or "Con Church."

We have, over the course of the last several years, had a strong presence at Dragon*Con and Con Nooga, resulting in a sizable membership in Georgia and Tennessee. We attend other cons as the availability and funds of our members allow.

We can be found at fansforchrist.org and on most popular social media platforms.

Appendix III: What is Misophonia?

Misophonia is a strong adverse reaction to certain sounds. It's not specifically an autistic trait but seems to frequently be a comorbidity with it as they share commonalities. Since I'm not a doctor and have no training, I can't provide clinical data regarding misophonia. What I can talk about is the effect it's had on me.

As an autie, I have a weakness when it comes to too much repetition. I don't want to give the impression that repetition is always a bad thing; the chorus of a good song or a catchy guitar riff can be welcome. The Living Sacrifice song "Conditional" is one of my favorite songs of all time. The last portion is instrumental with a repetitive rhythm and melody that are almost hypnotic. If it were another ten minutes long, I would sit entranced to the end. In this case, the effect is positive. I listen to a lot of classical music, movie soundtracks, and atmospheric bands like Midnight Syndicate while I write. Few, if any of them, cause me to stop what I'm doing to soak in the sounds like the droning of "Conditional" does.

"She Blinded Me with Science" by Thomas Dolby is an

example of a song that has the opposite effect. I can tolerate the song because I like the melody, but it's not one you'll find me listening to on purpose because I find the repetition annoying. I don't listen to a lot of the popular modern worship songs for the same reason. I've even gone so far as to request that our worship team not sing certain songs again because the repetition bothered me so much.

The aversion to repetition is one of the elements that may owe as much to me being an autie as it does to me being a misophonic (if you'll excuse my co opting an adjective as a noun). It's hard to say which condition has more to do with my reactions than the other, but I tend to think it's a combination of both.

You don't have to be autistic or misophonic to find repetition annoying, but my reactions to it can be extreme. I once listened to an audiobook that used the word "kitchen" like the author was getting paid every time he used it. If a character was at a table, it was the "kitchen table," if using the phone, it was the "kitchen phone," and so on throughout the entire book. If I'd been reading the story in print my eyes could have skipped over the repetition of the word. Since I was listening to a narrator read while I was driving, I couldn't escape the sound of the word.

That sort of repetition is like a pitcher of water: once it's full every additional drop spills over the side creating a bigger and bigger mess. The first few uses of the word "kitchen" didn't bother me. When I reached the point of too much repetition, every instance of the word felt like an assault. I finished the story because I couldn't stand walking away in the middle, but every time I heard the word I would react, sometimes as severely as screaming to try to cover the sound. For years after that I would tense up every time I heard someone say the word "kitchen."

I'll never watch the show "Lost in Space" from start to finish again because of similar reasons. I can't stand the frequency with which they say "Dr. Smith" - sometimes over and over for several minutes at a time (usually when another character is looking for him). No other character's name is repeated half as often as his, making me wonder why they would do that. I can't enjoy the show, certain episodes in particular, because of how much the repetition bothers me.

Certain sounds can have as much, if not more of an effect on me as repetition does. In those cases, the effect is usually immediate. Whispering is the most common sound with which I deal. I despise the sound of whispering. I have, on occasion, tried to make myself listen to ASMR (autonomous sensory meridian response) videos to see if I could desensitize myself to the sound of whispering, but I've never made thirty seconds into one of those without developing a headache severe enough to require medication.

In my most extreme reactions, I've tensed up so strongly I've broken what I was holding and have even drawn blood clawing at my ears because of sounds I couldn't escape. It's the severity of these reactions that set a misophonic apart from the average person.

Whispering may not be a trigger for everyone with misophonia. Many loud sounds, chewing, scratching, or clanking can have that same effect. The same loud guitars that soothe me may have the opposite reaction with another misophonic. If misophonia is part of your life, it's helpful to identify and avoid the sounds that elicit such negative reactions.

About the Author

Chad began writing when he found that he could make people laugh with silly poems. He combined that humor with his love for horror to write the award-winning Nightmare After Christmas and now enjoys building horror and fantasy worlds.

In the daylight hours he braves the working world of breaking software. When he's not working or writing, you'll often find him speaking on the topics of autism, writing, religion, and speculative fiction.

He lives just outside Atlanta with his wife and their four-legged children Red, Eliza, Hamilton, and Cthulhu. Guess which one of them he named.

Find him online at chadsides.com, on Instagram at chadsides.author, and on Facebook at chadsides.author.

Visit Dragonswalk Publishing at www.dragonswalk.com.

www.ingramcontent.com/pod-product-compliance
Lightning Source LLC
Chambersburg PA
CBHW030246130626
46549CB00002B/417